Keys to
Successful
Bible
Study

Keys to Successful Bible Study

How to Find God's Will in God's Word

John R. Martin
Introduction by John Sherrill

HERALD PRESS
Scottdale, Pennsylvania
Kitchener, Ontario
1981

Library of Congress Cataloging in Publication Data

Martin, John R., 1928-
  Keys to successful Bible study.

  Includes bibliographical references.
  1. Bible—study. I. Title.
BS600.2.M2   220'.07   81-6459
ISBN 0-8361-1963-0 (pbk.)   AACR2

KEYS TO SUCCESSFUL BIBLE STUDY
Copyright © 1981 by Herald Press, Scottdale, Pa. 15683
  Published simultaneously in Canada by Herald Press,
  Kitchener, Ont. N2G 4M5
Library of Congress Catalog Card Number: 81-6459
International Standard Book Number: 0-8361-1963-0
Printed in the United States of America
Design: Alice B. Shetler

81 82 83 84 85 86 87 88 10 9 8 7 6 5 4 3 2 1

To the many youth and adults
Who are seeking help
To understand the Bible
And to hear its message.

Contents

Introduction

When I began to read an advance copy of John Martin's *Keys to Successful Bible Study* my heart was warmed for a very special reason.

My wife, Elizabeth, and I have just returned from a trip into China. One of our most vivid impressions has to do with the Bible. For China is the only country we know of where a serious effort has been made to destroy every known copy of both the Old and the New Testaments.

To be clear-eyed, neither Elizabeth nor I feel that this campaign of the Cultural Revolution was especially aimed at Christians. Rather, the Red Guard set out to eliminate *anything* in Chinese culture that reflected a foreign influence. Christians were a target, but so were doctors and musicians and actors and professors who were too much touched by the West. Christians—and their Bible—suffered along with others.

But for whatever reason, Bibles were no longer approved. The Red Guard whose mission was to carry out the mandates of the Cultural Revolution would suddenly appear at a home and ask a lot of questions. Among these was, "Do you own a Bible?" If so, you'd better give a true answer, because if you said no and later a Bible was found in the house, the Red Guard simply killed you on the spot.

So the Christians in China came up with extraordinary tricks to help them keep in touch with God's Word. One boy with a photographic memory learned the entire New Testament. During the dark years of the Cultural Revolution, he was sent from village to village at the risk of his life to bring the memorized Word to believers. Another large Christian family, learning that the Red Guard was on its way, tore up its only Bible and handed out small portions to each member. "Stay awake all night. Read. Digest. Memorize passages. Then we will have to burn the Bible so that the Red Guard will not suspect what we've done. But the message will be in our hearts."

Today, as the Cultural Revolution has momentarily passed into history, there is a major effort to bring Bibles back into China. We have seen them there, small pocket-sized books that are, of course, enormously treasured because the people of China know what it is like to be without the Scripture. The Chinese today are studying the Word, memorizing, knowing the Bible, and knowing *about* the Bible. Never again will they be in a position where by a simple decree they are left without daily help from the written Word.

We need to take a lesson here. Not that the pattern of the Red Guard knocking on our doors and demanding our Bibles would be exactly echoed in our hometowns. The power of destruction is too subtle to repeat itself so precisely. But variations on this theme will certainly occur in land after land where first allegiance is demanded to some state, and where Christians are persecuted because they refuse to bow the knee. Almost inevitably when this happens believers are separated from their Bibles.

The reason is clear: the Bible is one of the Christian's very best, surest sources of strength. Take away one's Bible and a Christian is easier to maneuver. If there was one message which the Chinese believers asked us to bring back to the West it was this: Know your Bible. Memorize it. Treasure it. Study it.

A tool like John Martin's *Keys to Successful Bible Study* is invaluable in just this task. It is a clearly outlined, logical, brightly written guide to Scripture. Above all it is a book that helps us plant the Scripture in our daily lives so that we can better learn how to live in the dynamic dimension promised to us by the Lord.

John Sherrill
Chappaqua, N.Y.

Author's Preface

Jim was a typical church member. He attended Sunday morning worship services regularly, Sunday evening services occasionally, and Wednesday evening services several times a year. His involvement in other congregational activities was marginal and his general interest level in the Christian life was average.

On one occasion while making a pastoral call, Jim stated just how he felt about Bible study. "I enjoy studying the Bible at church," he said, "but I just don't get anything out of it when I try to study at home."

These words have rung in my ears for a number of years. They are lodged in my mind as a confession and a cry for help. They echo the felt frustration of many people today. "If the Bible is all that the church claims it to be, why doesn't it speak to me and my needs?"

Sally was a college freshman. She entered the Bible class with above average Bible knowledge and strong motivation. In the course, we both studied about the Bible and learned new ways of Bible study. One day after class, Sally shared the excitement she felt in studying the Bible for class assignments. "It seems like every word has become alive," she said. "I'm seeing truths I never saw before."

The contrast between Jim and Sally reflects the contrast between stagnant religious form and vibrant Christian living. It is the contrast between those who come to the biblical table and go away hungry and those who go away fed.

It is my conviction that God's written Word was intended for all of God's children. All who are able to read should find personal value in what they read. None needs go away empty.

In this book, I am attempting to bring together the needs I have discovered in congregations and the excitement I have experienced studying the Bible in the classroom. It is the fruit of a personal pilgrimage of experimenting with many methods both privately and in groups. Out of both successes and failures, there has emerged certain important understandings about the Bible and certain basic approaches to its study.

During my teenage years, general Bible reading met my needs. Later there was an urge to memorize both individual verses and selected chapters of the Scriptures. In seminary, I was introduced to Inductive Bible Study, a systematic, detailed approach. Some time later, I became aware of the value and importance of meditation. This pilgrimage has contributed to the writing of these chapters.

The book is divided into three parts. Part I attempts to encourage and direct Bible study by providing a clearer understanding of the Bible. Chapters one through four touch on our tragic biblical ignorance, God's intended purpose for the Bible, personal benefits received from meaningful study, and suggestions for understanding its message.

Before we can experience meaningful Bible study, we need to have some understanding of the Bible we study.

Every person brings to Bible reading or study certain ideas about the Bible. These ideas influence their attitude toward the Bible, their approach to studying its contents, and what they expect to have happen as a result of their study. Therefore, it is most important that we bring to our study of the Bible a solid understanding of this most special Book.

Part II identifies and explains four methods of Bible study that I have found to be both exciting and beneficial. Chapters five through eight deal with the methods of reading, meditation, memorization, and systematic study. I find in these four methods enough variety to provide a suitable approach for every person regardless of age or educational level.

I do not feel that one method is automatically better than another. Rather, each method has its own unique value. Each approach is best for a particular purpose and variety keeps freshness.

Most persons have an urge to experience something new. These creative urges are God-given and if followed can lead us closer to Him. Experimenting with these various approaches to Bible study can result in improving familiar methods and the excitement of new discoveries through new approaches.

Part III brings together key study aids that provide "handles" for the study process. Chapters nine through twelve provide a chart showing the key events of biblical history, identify chapters that speak uniquely to varied circumstances of life, provide information about each book of the Bible, and describe aids for biblical study. The material in this section is a resource to which you will want to refer again and again.

This book is designed to be used either privately or by small groups. The questions at the end of each chapter identify areas for personal reflection or for group discussion. Using these questions leads to greater self-understanding and growth.

Throughout the book, *The New International Version* of the Bible is used in most instances. When other versions are used, they are identified by initials following the Scripture reference.

I am indebted to many parishioners and students for their direct and indirect assistance in developing this material.

A special debt of gratitude is due my wife, Marian, for her aid in clarifying and typing the manuscript.

This book is written with the prayer that those who read it will be equipped to daily discover God's message in God's Word.

John R. Martin
Harrisonburg, Virginia

PART I
INSIGHTS FOR SUCCESSFUL STUDY

1

Many Bibles but Little Bible Knowledge

The Bible has often been described as the world's best-seller but also the world's least-read and least-understood book. How strange!

Think for a moment where you have seen Bibles during the past week. Perhaps on a book rack in the grocery store or at an airport. It may have been in a motel or hospital room. Or it might have been in your own living room or on your nightstand by your bed. A little like God, the Bible seems everywhere present.

Its availability is well known:

Over 1,630 languages and dialects now have the complete Bible or portions of it. These are the languages of 98 percent of the world's people.

2,000,000,000 copies of the Scriptures (Bibles, testaments, and smaller portions) have been distributed by the American Bible Society since its beginning in 1816.

191,000,000 copies of the Scriptures are distributed each year by the American Bible Society.

8,000,000 copies of *Good News for Modern Man,* Today's English Version of the New Testament, were sold the first year of publication, 1966. Nearly 60,000,000 copies are now in circulation.

1,200,000 copies of *The New International Version* were ordered by bookstores before the publication date and sales are running ahead of predictions.

At Cape Town, South Africa, a collection of all existing translations of the Bible is being safeguarded. It is assumed that Cape Town, on the southern tip of Africa, would escape the holocaust if a major nuclear war should erupt. The translations of the world's most translated book would thus be preserved.

Sounds impressive, doesn't it? And yet the Bible has been described as a seldom understood and frequently ignored book.

In a membership class for youth, we were studying about the Bible and its uniqueness. I decided to play a game.

"Suppose," I said, "a great tragedy would happen in our country and all the Bibles would be destroyed except the one you hold in your hands. Furthermore, no new copies could be printed. What price would you place on your Bible?"

The class thought in silence. Then one youth stated a price of one thousand dollars. Another quickly priced hers at one hundred thousand dollars. A third raised his price to one million dollars. Again there was silence. Then a fourth youth said she would not sell her Bible for any price. She would keep it and read it to others. Quickly the rest agreed.

"Fantastic," I said. "Since your Bible is so valuable, you likely read it daily and follow it carefully."

There was an uneasy silence, then an awkward smile, and finally a faint laugh. Why? How would you have reacted?

Many Neglect Bible Reading

Billy Graham has summarized our situation well when he stated, "One of the . . . greatest tragedies today is that, although the Bible is an available, open book, it is a closed book to millions—either because they leave it unread or because they read it without applying its teachings to themselves."[1]

A survey among the schoolchildren of New York revealed that 75 percent were unable to correctly identify the first four books of the Bible.

According to one survey, even people who claim to believe the Bible have a poor reading record. Only 12 percent read it every day, 34 percent read it once a week, and 42 percent read it occasionally.

Some creative writer dramatized this occasional reading in "A Bible Diary" that appeared in *Christian Guide*.

JANUARY: A busy time for me. Most of the family decided to read me through this year. They kept me busy for the first two weeks. They have forgotten me now.

FEBRUARY: My owner used me for a few minutes last week. He had been in an argument and was looking up some references.

MARCH: Grandpa visited us. He kept me on his lap for an hour reading 1 Corinthians 13.

APRIL: I had one busy day. My owner was appointed leader of something and used me. I got to go to church services for the first time this year—Easter Sunday.

MAY: I have a few green stains on my pages. Had some early spring flowers pressed in me.

JUNE: I look like a scrapbook. They have stuffed me full of clippings from the newspaper. One of the girls got married.

JULY: They put me in a suitcase today. I guess we are off on a vacation. I wish I could stay at home, as I will have to stay in this thing for a month.

AUGUST: Still in the suitcase.

SEPTEMBER: Back home again and in my old place. Have lots of company. Two "True Stories" and four "Funny Books" are on top of me. I wish I could be read as much as they are.

OCTOBER: They used me a little today. One of them is very sick. Right now I am shined up and in the center of the table. I think the preacher is coming.

NOVEMBER: Back in my old place.

DECEMBER: They are getting ready for Christmas, so I'll be covered under wrapping paper and packages.

While in college, a group of us students traveled one weekend to Richmond, Virginia, to help in a visitation program. During our stop at a restaurant, an employee asked who we were and where we were going. We took the opportunity to tell him about our Christian college and Christian service activities.

He listened with interest and then said, "I have a question I've always wanted to ask someone who has studied the Bible. How many years did it take Moses to go through the Red Sea?" We bit our lips to stop laughter, and explained the difference between Moses crossing the Red Sea and the 40 years of wilderness wandering. We decided he seldom read his Bible.

Why the Neglect?

An American Bible Society pamphlet reported a survey on "Why People Do Not Read the Bible." Twenty-two reasons were listed. The following seven reasons seem to be universal:

1. *The distracting tempo of our times* makes it difficult to find quiet places or moments of composure for daily reading of the Bible.

2. Many people *do not know the Bible is a living Book* to help solve life's daily problems.

3. Parts of the Bible are *difficult* to understand.

4. The Bible is a *large volume* and takes a long time to read from cover to cover.

5. Without guidance a new reader often starts at a place where he *becomes discouraged*.

6. The *language is unfamiliar,* and some words are hard to understand and interpret.

7. The Bible is *misrepresented* as an out-of-date, antique literary classic.[2]

If you are a "typical" person, you can say amen to most or all of these. And if these represent your thinking, you are certainly not alone.

Another way of explaining the neglect in Bible reading is to reflect on the attitudes of nonreaders. I have observed three basic attitudes reflecting three groups of persons.

Some Are Resistant

First, I have observed the attitude of resistance. This group is small in number. They are persons who have decided to keep the Bible at arm's length. They have deliberately decided to part company with the Scriptures. If they are faced with the question, "to read or not to read," their answer has already been determined. They are not willing to read. They are not interested. They would never agree with William Evans when he wrote, "The Bible is, without any exception, the most interesting book in the world."[3]

What has created this resistance? Perhaps they have been hurt by professing Christians. They may have had an unpleasant experience in a congregation. Or they may live with a gnawing sense of guilt. God is calling for confession but they resist. They are experiencing what David endured when he wrote in Psalm 32:3 and 4: "When I kept silent, my bones wasted away through my groaning all day long. For day and night your hand was heavy upon me; my strength was sapped as in the heat of summer."

For the resistant the sight of a Bible generates strong, negative feelings, a mental block.

Others Are Indifferent

A second attitude is indifference. This group is larger than the "resisters." They live with a don't care attitude. True, they know the biblical examples and admonitions urging attention to God's Word but they seem to be clothed in a cloak of indifference. Why bother? Why put forth the effort? I would like to know the Bible, but. . . .

Paul Little told about the student who asked his Bible teacher, "How can I know the Bible as well as you do?" The teacher replied, "It's easy, just study the Bible every day for fifty years." Reflecting on the incident, Little said, "There are no slick, painless methods by which we can grasp the Word of God. There is no pill we can take to make us effective Bible students. Study of anything takes work."[4]

For the indifferent, the work of study is unwelcomed.

Still Others Are Frustrated

Third, there is the attitude of frustration. This represents the largest group. Many people feel they should read their

Bible. They have read Paul's words to Timothy, "Do your best to present yourself to God as one approved, a workman who does not need to be ashamed and who correctly handles the word of truth" (2 Timothy 2:15). They have heard the preacher say, "You ought to." Their conscience says, "I ought to." So they do. A chapter a day keeps conviction away!

Out of a sense of duty or guilt they try. But nothing seems to happen. They do not understand. God does not seem to speak. They read words but not a message. They cannot understand the psalmist who meditated on the law "day and night" (Psalm 1:2), and who reported that God's words were "sweeter than honey to my mouth!" (Psalm 119:103).

After repeated failure, they give up in frustration. They feel locked outside God's place of blessing but cannot find the key that opens the door. It's not that they are resistant or indifferent. They love the Lord, and consider themselves followers of Christ. The needs of others concerns them. But the Word of God seems like a closed book. They wait in quiet desperation for someone to solve their frustrating dilemma.

I believe this attitude represents a large percentage of church members. Perhaps this is your inner feeling as you read these words.

But there is hope. In the book, *The Joy of Discovery*, author Oletta Wald confesses that at one time "I was a 'flounderer' in Bible study."[5] This book has helped many people.

The Bible was written for all people, not only for scholars. Many of the writers were ordinary people and they wrote for ordinary people. For several thousand years, the Bible has been widely read and will continue to be read until the end of time.

The book you are now reading is intended to introduce each reader to a general understanding of the Bible and various methods of Bible study, one of which will certainly fit you. I invite you to continue the pilgrimage with me, page by page, step by step.

QUESTIONS FOR REFLECTION OR DISCUSSION

1. If your Bible were to keep a diary, what story would it tell?

2. What prevents you from regular Bible reading or makes regular reading difficult?

3. Which of the three reader attitudes have you observed most frequently?

4. Which of the three reader attitudes do you identify with most closely? Why?

Notes

1. Henrietta C. Mears, *What the Bible Is All About* (Minneapolis: The Billy Graham Evangelistic Association, 1966), Preface.
2. *The Pastor and Ways of Using the Bible* (New York: American Bible Society), p. 25.
3. William Evans, *The Book of Books* (Chicago: The Bible Institute Colportage Association of Chicago, 1902), p. 11.
4. John B. Job, ed., *How to Study the Bible* (Downers Grove, Ill.: InterVarsity Press, 1972), p. 3.
5. Oletta Wald, *The Joy of Discovery* (Minneapolis: Bible Banner Press, 1956), Introduction.

A Unique Book

The Bible is the most unique book in the world. Agree? Disagree? Uncertain? Which?

Take a moment to complete the following sentence in twenty-five words or less. The Bible is the most unique book in the world because . . . .

Your reason for the Bible's uniqueness might have related to its sales record, its age, its author, its message, its prophecies, its claims for itself or its influence.

No doubt about it, the Bible is unique. But why?

Magical Uniqueness?
Some people see the Bible as a magical religious object. Having it with you brings good luck.

A night watchman in an Eastern city testified that he always carries a small New Testament in his shirt pocket because "it gives me strength."

One night while making rounds in the basement of a department store, he was shot in the chest by an intruder. The 22-caliber pistol bullet struck the New Testament and penetrated all but the back leather cover. The night watchman was knocked to the floor but suffered only a bruised chest.

As he leafed through his damaged New Testament, he told hospital employees that he has had the habit of carrying a Bible since he was baptized and this habit has saved his life.

A Pittsburgh, Pennsylvania, man applied the magical religious object attitude in a very ridiculous way. He was arrested after illegally entering a bank and setting off an alarm. Throughout the trial, he held his Bible and claimed, "Nothing is ever going to happen to me as long as I carry my Bible." In spite of his claim, he was found guilty of entering a bank with the intent of committing larceny.

The magical view is held by some people but not supported by the Bible itself.

Life Enriching Uniqueness

Many influential leaders have testified to the enrichment the Bible has brought to their own lives. Here are a few examples:

> George Washington said: "Only that conduct is really ethical that is the fruit of a tree whose roots are biblical principles."

> Abraham Lincoln stated about the Bible: "It is the best gift God has given to man. All the good Savior gave to the world was communicated through this Book. But for it we could not know right from wrong. All things desirable for man's welfare here and hereafter are to be found portrayed in it." Again he said, "Take all of this Book on reason that you can and the balance on faith, and you will, I am sure, live and die a happier man."

> Daniel Webster said in his later years: "I have read through the Bible many times. I now make it a practice to go through it once a year. It is the book of all others for lawyers

as well as for divines. I pity the man that cannot find in it a rich supply of thought and rules for his conduct. It fits a man for life. It prepares him for death."

John Wanamaker testified toward the end of his life: "Through the Holy Scriptures I found knowledge not to be obtained elsewhere, which established and developed fixed principles and foundations upon which all I am, and whatever I have done, are securely built and anchored. I found there faith . . . but more I found Christ . . . the Son of God endowed by His heavenly Father with power to transform character and human life." [1]

With testimonies like these, it is little wonder the Bible has been pictured in many graphic ways.

A Christian young man was packing to leave for college and carefully kept an empty space in his suitcase. A friend, observing the process, asked what was to go in that space. He replied, "A flashlight, a hammer, a sword, a map, and a mirror."

"But how," he questioned, "will you put all of those things in that little space?"

"Oh, that's easy. The space is for my Bible."

Testimonies of life enriching uniqueness only flow from the lips of persons who regularly read the Scriptures. In the deepest sense, the Bible is only valuable to us if read by us. Its message enriches the lives of Bible students, not Bible carriers.

Dr. Martin Niemoller, an outstanding church leader in Germany, spent over three years in a concentration camp for publicly opposing Nazi teachings. In prison his Bible was his most important possession and he repeated texts to unseen fellow prisoners who passed by his cell window. After the war, he spoke in a penetrating way about the importance of Bible reading and the influence it can have on our lives.

Addressing the British and Foreign Bible Society in

London, he raised two heart-searching questions which later appeared in a church bulletin:

> Do we read our Bible regularly every day? More than 52 years ago my father told me, "The Bible doesn't belong on the shelf but in your hand, under your eye, and in your heart." Do we need Jesus in our heart? Each one of us can give it only from his own experience. You can help each other by honestly expounding our experiences.

Dr. Niemoller concluded his address with a statement on the biblical value of the individual and the intended witness of the Christian church:

> God would never have allowed His Son to die for world progress or an earthly fatherland. It was for the individual people of the nations that God offered Him—that you and I might inhabit forever the new heaven and the new earth.... This witness we owe in love to the communists. I am disappointed that all over Christendom a spirit of fear is abroad; it is communism which ought to be afraid of Christianity.... We ought to be the salt of the earth and the light of the world!

When, like Dr. Niemoller, we put the Bible under our eye and in our heart, what do we find? What uniqueness appears in the Bible itself? I find three significant areas.

Uniqueness of Unity

It is obvious that your Bible is "a book." But the Bible has also been called "The Book." The term refers to its importance and value above other books. However, it also refers to the unique unity found in the total Scriptures from beginning to end. This unity is amazing because the Bible is really a library of many books. Have you counted them? They total 66 with 39 in the Old Testament and 27 in the New Testament.

The fact of this unity is also surprising because these 66 books were written over a period of about 1,500 years and there were about 40 different writers. Some were kings and some were shepherds. Some were scholars and some were fishermen.

But what is the unity that ties the 66 books together making it "The Book"? Bible scholars describe the unity with various terms but the term I like best is the word *redemption*.

What does the term mean? To redeem is to regain possession through the act of repurchasing.

Let me illustrate. Suppose someone would steal your camera and sell it to a camera shop. Eventually you would discover "your" camera at the shop and buy it from the shop owner. You would have regained possession through the act of repurchasing. The camera belonged to you, you lost the possession and ownership of it for a while, but eventually you bought it again. You redeemed it. The camera had "experienced" redemption.

The central theme of the Bible is God redeeming His people. God made man in His own image and for His own glory. God owned man by creation and He intended that all men and women live their lives in fellowship with Him. But through the temptation of Satan, man chose to go away from God thus renouncing God's ownership and breaking the fellowship. The story of the Bible is the story of God buying back man to Himself through the costly death of His son Jesus.

This story gives the Bible its unique unity. Each of the 66 books contribute in some way to this grand story. In fact, someone has observed that history is really His-story. It is the story of God redeeming His people. The Bible tells about this great act, an act so grand that the process is still going on today. All Christians are therefore redeemed people and should be able to understand the biblical account of man's need for redemption and God's provision for our redemption through Jesus, the Redeemer.

A student in a Bible class I was teaching shared with me an outline of the entire Bible focusing on the theme of redemption. A friend had given it to him. He gave it to me. I will pass it on to you. The outline illustrates the unity of the Scriptures found in the redemption theme.

> Genesis 1 to 11: Occasion of Redemption
> Genesis 12 to Malachi: Preparation for Redemption
> Matthew to John: Manifestation of Redemption
> Acts: Propagation of Redemption
> Romans to Jude: Explanation of Redemption
> Revelation: Consumation of Redemption

The Bible is the book of redemption. It is the Word of God because it is God's Word to mankind. True, it contains history but it is much more than history. It also contains the world's greatest literature, but it is much more than literature. Its uniqueness is found in the "scarlet thread" of redemption that runs through the heart of each of the 66 books making them one book.

Uniqueness of Author

How, you ask, was this unity achieved? How could so many authors writing over so many centuries have the same unique message? The answer lies in the uniqueness of the Bible's real Author.

Behind the earthly authors such as Moses, Isaiah, Paul, or John was the Divine Author, God Himself. All of the 40 writers of Scripture were directed by the Holy Spirit so that they wrote the message of God.

The English philosopher, John Locke, expressed this truth

quite vividly when he said of the Bible: "It has God for its Author, salvation for its end, and truth without any admixture of error for its matter. It is all pure, all sincere; nothing too much, nothing wanting."

The Apostle Peter describes the process even more graphically:

> Above all, you must understand that no prophecy of Scripture came about by the prophet's own interpretation. For prophecy never had its origin in the will of man, but men spoke from God as they were carried along by the Holy Spirit.
> —*2 Peter 1:20, 21*

There is the secret. The writers of Scripture wrote the message of God because they were moved by the Holy Spirit of God. True, the message came through human beings and what they wrote has their individual mark or characteristic. But their message was much more than their own. It was God's message, through God's messengers, to God's multitudes.

The Bible calls this process "inspiration." The term is based on two Greek words and literally means "God-breathed." Just as God breathed into the clay that He had formed and created man in His image, so God breathed into the select men that He had created and revealed both His will and Himself. This revelation we call the Bible.

Uniqueness of Purpose

To speak of God as the Author of the Bible does indeed make it unique. And to see the central theme of redemption gives the Bible a special unity. But one more level of uniqueness must be identified. The Bible is totally unequaled in its purpose and this purpose is overlooked by many Bible readers.

When plans were being made to send astronauts to the moon, some people believed the Bible could tell them whether or not the attempt would be successful. One man who approached the Bible in this way told me with great conviction that man would never reach the moon. Why? "Because the Bible says, 'The heaven, even the heavens, are the Lord's: but the earth hath he given to the children of men'" (Psalm 115:16, KJV). "There it is," he said, "that is proof."

Something went wrong with his Bible interpretation. Man did get to the moon. Was the Bible wrong or was the Bible being used for the wrong purpose? I would say the latter.

How do *you* read the Bible? For what purpose do you study it? The following poem begins to point the proper direction.

How Readest Thou?

It is one thing to read the Bible through,
Another thing to read to learn and do.
Some read it as their duty once a week,
But no instruction from the Bible seek;
Some read to bring themselves into repute
By showing others how they can dispute;
While others read because their neighbors do,
To see how long 'twill take to read it through.
Some read it for the wonders that are there—
How David killed a lion and a bear;
While others read it with uncommon care,
Hoping to find some contradictions there.
One reads with father's specs upon his head,
And sees the things just as his father said.
Some read to prove a preadopted creed;
Hence understand but little that they read,
For every passage in the book they bend
To make it suit that all-important end.
Some people read, as I have often thought,
To teach the book instead of being taught;
And some there are who read it out of spite—

I fear there are but few who read it right.
So many people in these latter days
Have read the Bible in so many ways
That few can tell which system is the best.
For every party contradicts the rest.
But read it prayerfully and you will see,
Although men contradict, God's words agree;
For what the early Bible prophets wrote,
We find that Christ and His apostles quote;
So trust no creed that trembles to recall
What has been penned by one and verified by all.
                    —Selected

What has been penned by one and verified by all? What is the purpose for which God intended the Scriptures?

The Apostle Paul stated the unique purpose of the Scriptures quite pointedly when he wrote to Timothy:

> But as for you, continue in what you have learned and have become convinced of, because you know those from whom you learned it, and how from infancy you have known the holy Scriptures, which are able to make you wise for salvation through faith in Christ Jesus. All Scripture is God-breathed and is useful for teaching, rebuking, correcting and training in righteousness, so that the man of God may be thoroughly equipped for every good work.
> *—2 Timothy 3:14-17*

The central purpose of the Scriptures is to lead us to faith in Christ Jesus which is the basis of salvation. The meaning of salvation is similar to redemption, the term we examined earlier in the chapter.

But Paul defines still further the unique purpose of the Bible. It is profitable or useful for teaching, rebuking, correcting, and for training in righteousness. Each term has special meaning and together they reveal a lifelong process.

Teaching refers to instructing us in the Christian faith. The Scriptures tell us all we need to know in order to have faith in Christ Jesus. They set forth the plan of salvation. The instruction to repent of sin and to turn in faith to.Christ may sound very simple. But what other book or writings instruct us in this important message. The Bible is unique because it points us to Christ, the Savior of the world.

The term rebuke means to refute or correct error. A further purpose of the Scriptures is to correct our false understandings about God's truth. Every person, both Christian and non-Christian has some false ideas or opinions about God and His way of seeing life and the world. Our understandings may be accurate but they are never totally complete in this life. The Scriptures are intended to correct or clarify our understandings. Many of the New Testament Epistles were written to correct some heresy or erroneous belief. These letters perform the special purpose of rebuking our human opinions.

Correcting refers to amending our ways or giving proper guidance. It portrays the picture of resetting the direction of our lives. Jesus spoke about the broad way that leads to destruction and the narrow way that leads to life. The specific purpose of the Scriptures is to get us on the right path. It is to turn our feet from the broad road of death to the narrow road of life. This is the task of correcting.

Training in righteousness relates to instruction in moral discipline. The phrase refers to directing our lives so that they conform to the will of God in purpose, thought, and action. It is an inclusive term covering the active duties of the religious life. Paul may have had in mind such spiritual disciplines as worship, prayer, and witness. Again, this is a unique purpose.

In summary, the unique purpose of the Bible is to start us in the Christian faith, to correct our understandings of God's truth, to get us on God's narrow path, and to keep us walking on that eternal road until we meet Christ. When this happens in our lives, we are equipped for every good work God calls us to perform.

I have heard the Bible used to support racism, to justify warfare and poverty, and to excuse immoral living. How tragic. The purpose of the Bible was being perverted to support man's perverted desires. The intended purpose described by Paul should be clearly in our minds as we study the Bible.

Truly the Bible is a very unique book. It provides for us that which no other book can provide. It provides what God wants every person to know. Is it any wonder that William Lyon Phelp, a noted professor of English literature, concluded that "a knowledge of the Bible without a college course is more valuable than a college course without a knowledge of the Bible."[2]

QUESTIONS FOR REFLECTION OR DISCUSSION

1. Do you believe the Bible as a book has magical value? Give your reasons for your answer.

2. In what ways has your life been enriched through the message of the Scriptures? Which of the testimonies comes closest to your own?

3. Identify themes of unity running through the Scriptures in addition to redemption. Which of these themes do you feel best ties the Scriptures together?

4. For what questionable purposes have you observed the Bible being used?

Notes

1. Walter C. Erdman, *Sources of Power in Famous Lives* (Cokesbury Press), quoted in Sibyl Brame Townsend, *Bible Study* (Nashville: Broadman Press, 1940), pp. 25, 26.
2. Edward P. Blair, *The Bible and You* (Nashville: Abingdon Press, 1953), pp. 8, 9.

3

Benefits of Bible Study

The benefits of Bible study can be as varied as God's blessings and as broad as His love. What we can receive from studying God's Word is as vast as God Himself. Through God's Word we come to know Him and life with Him has few limits.

If you want an interesting experience, ask several persons who study the Bible what benefits they receive from their study. All persons study the same Bible but those who know God most intimately reap the greatest rewards. A deep, personal knowledge of God and a profound appreciation of His Word seem to go together.

The psalmist both knew about God through personal experience and also knew the rich benefits of studying His Word. Notice how he relates these two realities.

> Oh, how I love your law!
>   I meditate on it all day long.
> Your commands make me wiser than my enemies,
>   for they are ever with me.
> I have more insight than all my teachers,
>   for I meditate on your statutes.

I have more understanding than the elders,
　　for I obey your precepts.
I have kept my feet from every evil path
　　so that I might obey your word.
I have not departed from your laws,
　　for you yourself have taught me.
How sweet are your promises to my taste,
　　sweeter than honey to my mouth!
I gain understanding from your precepts;
　　therefore I hate every wrong path.
　　　　　　　　　　　　　—Psalm 119:97-104

Discoveries of this nature have happened among many followers of God since the days of the psalmist. D. L. Moody placed on the flyleaf of his Bible a most significant statement about the Scriptures. We do not know who wrote these words but we do know that the person, like the psalmist, knew God intimately and the benefits that can come from studying the Bible.

This Book contains the Word of God, the state of man, the way of salvation, the doom of sinners, and the happiness of believers.

Its doctrines are holy, its precepts are binding, its histories are true, and its decisions immutable.

Read it to be wise, believe it to be safe, and practice it to be holy. It contains light to direct you, food to support you, comfort to cheer you.

It is the traveler's map, the pilgrim's staff, the pilot's compass, the soldier's sword, and the Christian's charter.

Here paradise is restored, heaven opened, and the gates of hell disclosed.

Christ is the grand object, our good its design, and the glory of God its end.

It should fill the memory, rule the heart, and guide the feet.

Read it slowly, frequently, prayerfully.

It is a mine of wealth, a paradise of glory, a river of judgment.

It is given you in life, will be opened at the judgment, and be remembered forever.

It involves the highest responsibility, will reward the greatest labor, and condemns all who trifle with its sacred contents.
   —Found on the flyleaf of Moody's Bible.

This statement identifies a number of interesting benefits. Many more could be added. I will identify four primary benefits I have observed and experienced.

A *Vital Christian Life*

It is through the Bible that we learn about Jesus. He said that the Scriptures "testify about me" (John 5:39). It is through Jesus that we receive new life, for He said, "I have come that they may have life, and have it to the full" (John 10:10b). Again Jesus said "I am the way and the truth and the life. No one comes to the Father except through me" (John 14:6).

The Apostle Paul related the same truth to Timothy when he wrote that "from infancy you have known the holy Scriptures, which are able to make you wise for salvation through faith in Christ Jesus" (2 Timothy 3:15).

Peter took this truth one step further when he instructed, "Like newborn babies, crave pure spiritual milk, so that by it you may grow up in your salvation" (1 Peter 2:2).

William Evans summarized this biblical truth when he said, "The Bible has life-giving power. As we read it, we know there is in it a Spirit that speaks to our spirit, a Life that touches our life. As we believe it, we are 'born again . . . by the Word of God, which liveth and abideth forever.' "[1]

One uncomparable benefit then of Bible study is discovering new life in Christ and "growing up" in our salvation. How tragic it is when we fail to experience this benefit either because we don't read the Bible or because we don't respond to its invitation to life. We can live beside the source of spiritual life and choose spiritual death instead.

In her book, *Men as Trees Walking,* Margaret T. Apple-garth tells about a most instructive experiment conducted by the French scientist, Jean Henri Fabre. He discovered that the processionary caterpillar had an unbelievable tendency to crawl in circles following a leader. An experiment was arranged to determine how rigidly they would follow that instinct. Here is her description of what happened.

> Knowing that their only necessary food was pine needles from their natural habitat, the pine trees, he filled up a flowerpot to the brim with fresh needles; and then arranged his caterpillars in a circle around the rim of this same pot, their front ends against the backs of the caterpillars ahead; their food readily accessible within a mere fraction of an inch.
>
> Immediately they started their tireless procession, going around and around and around without once stopping, day or night, even for food. He was fascinated to find that they kept up this monotonous marathon one day; two days; three; four; five; and even six. But on the seventh day they all died—from sheer exhaustion, and from lack of food, of course: although their necessary nourishment was only a hairbreadth away; a mere turning of the head, and they could have lived. But they were frantically intent on this reckless ritual of revolving.
>
> Pine trees are still full of them.
>
> And pews, also![2]

Jesus would have us learn the lesson of the caterpillars. They crawled to their death beside the source of life. We may be running to our death with the source of life in our hands.

What causes the rejection of an eternal benefit? Likely it is sin in one form or another. D. L. Moody was quite right when he said of the Bible, "This book will keep you from sin or sin will keep you from this book."

I have observed people who cuddled their pet sins even though those unconfessed sins were bringing great harm to their own lives. In the process, they had lost their hunger for the Word.

I have seen others who clung to their unforgiving attitudes somehow feeling they were thereby hurting the other person. Actually they were hurting only themselves.

These persons were failing to embrace the benefit of a vital Christian life. They were the losers.

Dynamic Christian Living

Life is for living. Christ does not merely give us new life so that we will be alive, He gives us new life so that we can live life with all of its fullness. A second benefit of Bible study is living with a supernatural dynamic. It is great to be alive. It is even greater to be experiencing the full potential of life with Christ.

The level of our involvement with the Scriptures determines the level of our spiritual nourishment. And the level of our spiritual nourishment determines the level of our spiritual vitality. Christians who neglect the Word suffer from spiritual malnutrition. They are spiritually anemic.

How much better it is to have the spiritual vigor of an athlete. How much better it is to radiate health and success rather than sickness and failure.

Charles E. Jefferson described the relationship between the Bible and our own lives in the following words: "The Bible is a world power, and we release the power only as we read and ponder and incarnate the great truths which are set forth in its pages."[3]

The psalmist knew the benefit of dynamic living made possible through the Word. Picture his imagery in your mind and compare it with your own life.

Blessed is the man
  who does not walk in the counsel
    of the wicked
or stand in the way of sinners
  or sit in the seat of mockers.
But his delight is in the law of the
      Lord,
    and on his law he meditates day
      and night.
He is like a tree planted by streams of
    water,
    which yields its fruit in season
and whose leaf does not wither.
    Whatever he does prospers.

                              —*Psalm 1:1-3*

The prosperity about which the psalmist spoke can still be experienced today.

Dr. Edward L. R. Elson who has served as pastor of the National Presbyterian Church, Washington, D.C., and as chaplain of the United States Senate told about the way he experienced the blessing and prosperity of God.

As a young minister, he took three vows:

1. He would keep the spiritual discipline of a meaningful devotional life at all cost, out of his love for God.
2. He would keep alive all of the creative power God had given him so that his ministry would be fresh and vital.
3. He would keep all bitterness and resentment out of his life. Envy and jealousy would be spiritual poison to his soul.

After years of ministry and service, Dr. Elson observed that when he kept the first vow or a meaningful devotional life, the others naturally followed. God kept alive his creative powers for ministry and removed resentments from his life. But when he failed to keep the first vow, he failed in the others as well.

What Dr. Elson discovered has been experienced and expressed by many others. Alfred P. Gibbs wrote, "No one can begin the day well, go on well, or end up well, who fails to make provision for this 'quiet time' with God."[4]

A professional violinist once commented that if she failed to practice one day, she could tell it. If she failed to practice for two days, her music critics could tell it. And if she failed to practice for three days, the whole world could tell it. Apparently being a professional musician and a dynamic Christian have some similarities.

The possibilities of living dynamically are within the grasp of each person and the potential blessings sound most attractive. Why then do so many of us fail to achieve?

Some fail because they give up during the valley experiences of life. When they feel down, they quit. They give up what could take them up out of the valley. When they need spiritual strength the most, they desire it the least. They forget that all Christians have some valley experiences and that the quickest way up to dynamic Christian living is through their faithful feeding on spiritual food.

Others try to feed their souls when their bodies and minds are tired and fatigued. Normally this does not work. They may have the satisfaction of faithfully reading the Bible but they do not have the blessing of receiving the benefits. We should be mentally alert to reap the greatest results.

Throughout the centuries, the people of God have experienced dynamic Christian living when they fed on the daily spiritual meat of God's Word. This is a blessing available to all of God's children regardless of their vocation or situation in life.

Awareness of God's Will
Those who believe in Christ are called Christians. To be

called a Christian means that we are Christ's disciples. He is our teacher. But it also means that we are Christ's followers. He is our Leader.

Jesus said it quite plainly. "My sheep listen to my voice; I know them, and they follow me" (John 10:27).

How can we hear His voice so we can follow? How can we become aware of God's will?

Our words reveal who we are and what we are thinking. God's Word reveals who He is and what He wants us to know. We can hear His voice and discover His will as we reflect on His Word. Isaiah had this confidence when he said, "Whether you turn to the right or to the left, your ears will hear a voice behind you, saying, 'This is the way; walk in it' " (Isaiah 30:21).

But, you ask, how does God speak through His Word to reveal His will? God usually shows us His will through general principles taught in the Scriptures. If you wish to know God's will concerning a job, you will not find in the Scriptures a command to be a factory employee, a construction worker, or a schoolteacher. Neither will the Bible tell you which factory to choose, which construction job to select, or in which school to teach. Rather, the Bible will give you important principles to help in making such choices.

The Apostle Paul mentions some of these guiding principles. "For we are God's workmanship, created in Christ Jesus to do good works, which God prepared in advance for us to do" (Ephesians 2:10). What is the principle? Before we were born, God had a purpose for us, a plan for our lives. We seek God's will because we know He has a plan for us and wants to lead us into it.

There is another principle that becomes a little more specific. "And whatever you do, whether in word or deed, do it all in the name of the Lord Jesus, giving thanks to God the Father through him" (Colossians 3:17). What is this principle? God wants both our words and deeds to be consistent with His name or character. God has called us to live for His praise and glory. Any job that He could approve could be a potential job for us. But a job that He could not approve would fail to bring Him glory.

Beyond the principles of these two Scriptures, we should look at our inner sense of calling and our gifts and abilities. Sharing with other Christians often helps us find God's direction.

There are times, however, when God chooses to reveal His will very specifically through the Scriptures.

I grew up on a small dairy farm. As a teenager, I enjoyed animals, machinery, and the out-of-doors, and wanted someday to own my own farm. But God was also speaking to me about a life of Christian service. There was a deep inner call to become a minister. After high school, this call became stronger and expanded to include an urge to attend college.

An intense inner struggle raged. I wanted to farm. Furthermore, I was needed on the farm. My brothers were not interested in farming and chose other employment. My father spent most of his time with a small stove business and depended on me to operate the farm.

However, God's urging to begin Bible study continued. The struggle intensified. If I went to college, who would operate the farm? If I did not go to college, would I be prepared for what might lay ahead in ministry?

Unexpectedly God spoke specifically through the Scriptures. It happened in Sunday school class. The lesson was on Christ's call of His disciples. During the class period, I read these words:

As Jesus walked beside the Sea of Galilee, he saw Simon

and his brother Andrew casting a net into the lake, for they were fishermen. "Come, follow me," Jesus said, "and I will make you fishers of men." At once they left their nets and followed him. When he had gone a little farther, he saw James son of Zebedee and his brother John in a boat, preparing their nets. Without delay he called them, and they left their father Zebedee in the boat with the hired men and followed him.   —Mark 1:16-20

As I pondered this passage, God suddenly seemed to say, "John, here is your answer." The message was unmistakeable. Jesus was calling disciples to follow Him for ministry. He was calling me too. One of the men called was named John. That was my name too. John was working with his father in a business. So was I. John, the disciple, left his father with the *hired men* and followed. There was the answer. If the dairy farm was to continue operating, there could be a hired man. John left and followed. I must too.

In a few minutes, the struggle was over. God had made His will plain. He had shown the way and I would walk in it. This experience made me aware of God's will. It was a major turning point in my life.

In the years that have passed, I have discovered that many people go through life without a clear knowledge of God's will. Some have not listened for the direction of God. Others have listened but the direction has not come because their will was not surrendered. They wanted their will to become God's will rather than wanting God's will to become their own.

The keys to hearing are listening and surrendering. Then God is free to speak. He will if we do not give up the search.

Effective Christian Witness
We have now come a full circle. First, we noticed that the message of the Bible opens to us a new life through Christ.

Then, if we continue the spiritual pilgrimage, we will experience dynamic Christian living. This will result in our discovering and doing God's will. Finally, His will always involves some work or witness regardless of our vocation. Here again, the Bible is vitally important. It is absolutely necessary. So at every stage of life, the Bible is relevant, important, and necessary.

Paul, the apostle, knew personally the importance of the Scriptures for an effective Christian witness. Writing to the young man Timothy he instructed:

> Command and teach these things. Don't let anyone look down on you because you are young, but set an example for the believers in speech, in life, in love, in faith and in purity. Until I come, devote yourself to the public reading of Scripture, to preaching and to teaching. Do not neglect your gift, which was given you through a prophetic message when the body of elders laid their hands on you. Be diligent in these matters; give yourself wholly to them, so that everyone may see your progress. Watch your life and doctrine closely. Persevere in them, because if you do, you will save both yourself and your hearers. *1 Timothy 4:11-16.*

The Scriptures, his life, and his witness were all interrelated. An effective witness would grow out of a nurtured, consistent life. This in turn would grow out of a serious use of the Word.

George Mueller was well known as a man who gave serious attention to the Scriptures and who in turn had a significant ministry to orphans in England. He also had an effective witness to men and women in England and in other countries where he spoke. Mueller observed that when we discover God's truth through personal Bible study, God always gives us an opportunity to pass that truth on to others. And isn't that the essence of witness—telling what we have experienced and discovered?

When you study the lives of great Christians, you discover that they were ordinary people who became extraordinary witnesses through God's special touch on their lives. They were people who knew deeply the importance and benefit of Bible study. You cannot understand the significant witness of persons of the past like Martin Luther or John Wesley apart from their involvement with the Scriptures.

If you identify Christians today whose witness is effective for Christ, you will discover persons who have a regular exposure to the Word and its message. Your mind may turn to Joni Eareckson or Corrie ten Boom. John Chrysostom, a church leader of the fourth century, was right when he said that the Bible is to the Christian what a tool is to the builder.

God does not promise fame or popularity if we faithfully study His Word, but He does promise to prosper our lives and this includes our witness.

QUESTIONS FOR REFLECTION OR DISCUSSION

1. What personal application came to your mind as you read about the processionary caterpillars?

2. Have you made any vows similar to those of Dr. Elson? What are some vows God is asking you to make now?

3. Are you aware of actions or attitudes that dim your desire for spiritual food? Jesus would like you to give them to Him.

4. How clear are you about God's will for your life? How closely are you following His will?

Notes

1. Evans, op. cit., p. 12.
2. Margaret T. Applegarth, *Men as Trees Walking* (New York: Harper & Brothers, 1952), p. 54.

3. Charles E. Jefferson, *The Bible in Our Day* (Oxford University Press), quoted in Townsend, op. cit., p. 13.
4. Alfred P. Gibbs, *The Quiet Time* (tract) (Westchester, Ill.: Good News Publishers), p. 4.

4

Clues to Understanding

The Bible has been unused, misused, and abused. It has been unused by those who felt it was irrelevant and useless. It has been misused by those who wanted to make it speak their message. It has been abused by those who failed to understand its intended message and made light of it through their own ignorance.

During college days, I spent a summer near Gulfport, Mississippi, helping at a mission church. One evening I went to a rural home to visit a family that my pastor had learned to know. The family members wore the scars of sin and warped religion. They needed some sound Bible teaching.

When I arrived at the home, I met a pastor from another congregation who announced that he had come to conduct a Bible study. I decided to stay and take part in the meeting.

After a small group gathered, the pastor identified 2 Corinthians 5 as the chapter for study. In this passage, we have Paul's testimony that he does not fear death because he will be present with the Lord when he leaves this body. The pastor, however, had his own message in mind. He emphasized verse 6 which reads: "Therefore we are always confident, knowing that, whilst we are at home in the body, we are absent from the Lord" (2 Corinthians 5:6, KJV).

"This means," said the pastor, "that when we stay at home on Sunday morning, we are absent from the Lord. The only way we can be present with the Lord is to go to church on Sunday morning."

He then proceeded to urge attendance at his church the following Sunday.

Obviously the Bible was being misused. This pastor was altering its message for his own purpose. Knowingly or unknowingly, he was misinterpreting the Scriptures.

The Bible has also been abused. Some time ago I had contact with a government official in Washington, D.C., who had never read the Bible. At the urging of a friend, he started at Genesis and read through the Old Testament. When he finished the last book, Malachi, he reported to the friend on his impression.

"I wouldn't call that book holy," he said. "The only thing I found was war and sex." The friend urged him to continue reading, believing that the New Testament would change his conclusion.

It is true that there is war and sex in the Old Testament but there is also much more. Out of his own ignorance, the government official was abusing the Bible. He, along with the Southern pastor, needed some clues for understanding.

A proper understanding of the Bible involves what we are as persons and our grasp of basic principles of interpretation. Both of these areas are vitally important. Some people lack in both areas; others lack in one area. We study the Bible as a total person. Study involves the heart and the mind. We bring to Bible study our own spiritual condition and our ideas on how it should be interpreted.

Bible study is therefore different from the study of other

books. The spiritual condition of the heart does not directly affect the study of mathematics or history, but it does directly affect the study of the Scriptures.

What then are some clues for understanding the Bible?

Know Christ Personally

Before we can understand spiritual truth, we must be spiritually alive. Nicodemus was a religious leader in Jesus' day but he had not become spiritually alive through faith in Christ as the Messiah. He did not know Christ personally. Jesus told him that "unless a man is born again [from above], he cannot see the kingdom of God" (John 3:3b).

Jesus identified a most important clue to understanding. The message of the Bible or spiritual truth can only be understood by spiritual persons.

Paul, the apostle, had the same reality in mind when he told the church at Corinth: "The man without the Spirit does not accept the things that come from the Spirit of God, for they are foolishness to him, and he cannot understand them, because they are spiritually discerned" (1 Corinthians 2:14).

Why, you ask, must we be spiritually alive to understand spiritual truth? When you know Christ personally, reading the Bible is like reading a letter from a personal friend. You understand what is written because you know the person who wrote it. A letter from a stranger with an intimate message is difficult to read because you do not know the person.

Last Christmas, I found a meditation on the back of a Christmas card that states this truth in descriptive terms.

The Incarnation
The Bible is the *written* Word of God.

> The Christ is the *living* Word of God.
> The divinely intended contrast is striking. Both are
> revelations of God's heart and mind. The Bible is a product
> of the Holy Spirit and submissive human authors. The
> Christ is the product of the Holy Spirit and a submissive
> Jewish maiden who bore Him.
>
> The Scriptures are referred to as the holy Bible, and Christ is
> referred to as the holy Child. *Christmas is God becoming*
> *flesh to speak to man face-to-face.* His message can be found
> only in one volume, the Bible—the eternal, unchanging
> Word of God

The government official had not gotten acquainted with
Christ, the living Word of God, so he failed to understand
the Bible, the written Word of God.

Prepare Your Heart to Listen

When we study the Bible to find our own message, we
usually fail to hear God's message. To hear, we must listen.
Since the Bible is God's Word to mankind, we should read
expecting God to speak His message to us. This means we
should listen with the attitude of reverence and respect.

Suppose Christ would return to earth in a physical body
and would have an appointment to meet you at 7:00 p.m.
tomorrow evening. How would you prepare for the meeting
and with what attitude would you enter His presence?

Certainly you would pray that God would prepare your
heart and mind to receive His message. You would want to
be spiritually alert.

Also, you would deal with any known sin in your life. If
you were living with unconfessed and unforgiven sin, it
would be a barrier to your fellowship. The words of the
prophet Isaiah would likely ring in your ears. "Your sins
have hidden his face from you, so that he will not hear"
(Isaiah 59:2).

Finally, you would meet Christ with an attitude of reverence and respect. His words to you and His presence with you would be your most important concern. He would receive your total attention.

You would meet Christ after preparation and with anticipation. You would then leave, knowing you had met God. Without heart preparation and the attitude of reverence, you would likely fail to hear God's message. Even though His message would be given, you would not hear it. These same areas of preparation are important when we want to meet Christ through the pages of Scripture.

Practice Obedience

When Jesus taught the crowds, some of the people understood His message and some did not. All of them heard His words but many did not understand the message He was speaking. One of the groups that usually failed to understand was the Pharisees. On one occasion, Jesus told some of them who believed, "If you continue in my word, you are truly my disciples, and you will know the truth, and the truth will make you free" (John 8:31, 32, RSV).

The message of the Bible is for people with an active commitment to knowing and doing truth, not for those who want to be spectators in the bleachers. Peter adds his words to those of Jesus, when he speaks of people who "have purified yourselves by obeying the truth so that you have sincere love for your brothers" (1 Peter 1:22).

The sixteenth-century Anabaptist leader, Hans Denck, stated the same truth in vivid words when he said, "No man can know Christ truly unless he follows him daily in life."

Normally Christ does not reveal new truth until we start living the truth we already know. Many Christians want to be spiritual giants but they fail to take the first step in spiritual growth, namely, the step of obedience to the truth they already understand.

Peter Marshall provided some helpful insight when he observed that the passages of Scripture that cause us the most problems are not those we cannot understand. Rather, they are the passages we well understand but do not want to follow.

Expect the Holy Spirit to Teach You

The best interpreter of any book is its author. In chapter two, we observed that the primary author of the Scriptures is the Holy Spirit (2 Peter 1:21). This process we called inspiration. The Holy Spirit, being the author, is also involved in interpretation. This process is called illumination. It happens when the Holy Spirit makes the Scriptures alive and understandable. When the Holy Spirit teaches us the meaning of biblical truths, illumination is happening.

G. W. Bromiley stated that illumination is "an unavoidable implicate" of inspiration. He also said, "Without the Holy Ghost it [the Bible] can be read only on the level of the human letter. What is given by the Spirit must be read in the Spirit."[1]

In the early church, there were false teachers who denied that Jesus was truly human, that he was truly a man. They concluded that Jesus could not be the Messiah. They also taught that Salvation comes through superior knowledge, not faith in Jesus. To these people John wrote:

> I am writing these things to you about those who are trying to lead you astray. As for you, the anointing you received from him remains in you, and you do not need anyone to teach you. But as his anointing teaches you about all things and as that anointing is real, not counterfeit—just as it has taught you, remain in him.
> —*1 John 2:26, 27*

The anointing about which John wrote was the ministry of the Holy Spirit teaching them that Jesus was truly God and truly man—that He was the Savior of the world. The Holy Spirit still teaches us the same truth as we read the Scriptures because they testify to who Jesus is (John 5:39).

A deep thrill of my life has been to fellowship with Christians who have little academic training but who have a profound understanding of the Scriptures. They have studied in the school of biblical meditation with the Holy Spirit as their Teacher.

Another thrilling experience is to have the Holy Spirit apply truth to your own life situation causing the Scriptures to become alive and personal. The Holy Spirit wants to participate actively in our Bible study. He wants to reveal the truths of God's Word to God's people.

Place the New Testament Above the Old

The Washington government official whom I mentioned earlier did not understand the proper relationship between the Old and New Testaments. He assumed that since the Old Testament had frequent references to war and sex, the New Testament would also. This is called a "flat book" view of Scripture. It views both Testaments on an equal level morally and spiritually.

A better way to view the Scriptures is to recognize the fact of progressive revelation. God always revealed Himself to men and women where they were, at the level of their understanding. Therefore, there was a progression in the message God shared with mankind.

The Old Testament contains many prophecies. The New Testament contains their fulfillment. The Old Testament deals in promise. The New Testament reveals the reality that was promised. The Old Testament tells about God preparing a people for Himself, the people of God. The New Testament tells about the Messiah coming through the people of God to bring salvation to the people of the world.

Christ is the final revelation of God to man. In Him we find the Old Testament prophecies fulfilled. In Him we find the highest ethical and spiritual teaching. In Him we find God among us. His revelation is both the highest and the final. God has not promised any additional or higher revelation. Eternity will be a further learning of the truth Christ has already taught.

What value then is the Old Testament? It has a value all its own, but it is also necessary for understanding the New Testament. Someone has packed a lot of truth in a few words when he wrote the following lines:

> The New is in the Old contained,
> The Old has in the New remained.

Many key truths of the Bible are found in seed form in the Old Testament. Then they blossom forth as full-grown plants in the New Testament. Jesus said, "Do not think that I have come to abolish the Law or the Prophets; I have not come to abolish them but to fulfill them" (Matthew 5:17). His coming completed all that the law anticipated. Therefore, the New is contained in the Old and the Old remains in the New. Like Siamese twins with one heart, they are inseparable.

The Bible then is something like a house. The Old Testament is like the foundation and the New Testament is like the living area and roof. Both the living area and roof rest on the foundation and are greatly influenced by it. To understand the total house you must understand the foundation as well as the rest of the building. But we should not forget that the ethical and spiritual teachings by which we are called to live come from the roof rather than the foundation. They come from the compassionate love of Jesus rather than the wars of the Old Testament.

Examine the Historical Setting

The books of the Bible were written to a particular people at a particular time, yet they were also written for all peoples of all times. Because they were written in a specific historical setting, we need to study them in the light of that setting. And because they contain a timeless message, we need to study them for their instructions to us.

Of course, the Bible has spoken to millions of people who were unable to study Bible history. But a study of Bible history always enriches your study of the Scriptures.

As a young Christian, I recall reading Jesus' warning and instructions concerning the destruction of Jerusalem (Matthew 24). I could not understand why this was to be such a significant event. Later while studying Bible history, I learned that the predicted destruction came only 40 years after the death of Jesus or in AD 70. Furthermore, there was an enormous loss of life. Thousands of Jews were slain and thousands were taken captive. In addition, this event marked the end of the Jewish sacrificial system. Jews have not offered sacrifices at a temple since that day. No wonder the event was so significant in Jesus' mind.

A study of Bible history can also help us understand some of the obscure passages. For example, Deuteronomy 14:21b. "Do not cook a young goat in its mother's milk."

Why was this command given? Why was this a sinful act? Biblical history tells us that this act was a pagan worship ritual. Since Israel was to worship only the true God, Jehovah, they were not to observe pagan religious practices. This could lead them to worship the pagan god.

Christianity is a historical faith. It is rooted in God's acts in history. The Bible is a historical book. It tells us what God did in history. Therefore, history becomes a window through which we can more clearly see the biblical message.

Let the Scriptures Explain Themselves

It has been said that the Bible is its own best interpreter. As we read the Bible and have questions about the meaning of its teachings, the first place to look for the answer is right within the Scriptures. This is a very sound approach and it can be applied in several ways.

We should look for an explanation within the passage. At times the biblical writers anticipated the questions of the readers and provided the answers. In 1 Corinthians 15, Paul presented his most detailed discussion of the resurrection of Christ and the followers of Christ. In verse 35, he identified their questions about how the dead will be raised and the kind of body they will have. These questions were then answered in the remainder of the chapter.

We should also look for an explanation to our questions in related passages. Since various books of the Bible provide teaching on the same subjects, questions raised in one passage may be answered in another.

There are many passages in the Bible dealing with prayer. One that is often misunderstood is: "You may ask me for anything in my name, and I will do it" (John 14:14). Does Jesus mean that we can ask to live to be 150 years old or to suddenly have a million dollars and He will answer our prayer? Hardly. Jesus has more to say about prayer in chapters 15 and 16 of John. Here we find certain conditions such as our abiding in Him and His words abiding in us (John 15:7). As the Word of God abides in us, we learn to understand God's will and way of working in our lives. We will then ask according to the will and purpose of God.

Finally, we should look for an explanation to our questions through careful reading. Many verses are misquoted and they give a warped view of the Bible's real message. How often have you heard the statement, "Money is the root of all evil"? It is implied that this represents the biblical teaching. Actually the Bible says, "For the love of money is a root of all kinds of evil" (1 Timothy 6:10a). Money can be used for many good purposes. But the love of money can lead to many evil actions.

The Scriptures do, in a wonderful way, explain themselves. Therefore, the more we know about the Bible, the greater will be our ability to understand its teachings.

Check with Other Christians

Throughout the Bible you see God's people living together in community. You find the preaching of the gospel leading to the development of a new people. Peter declared this truth when he wrote, "Once you were not a people, but now you are the people of God" (1 Peter 2:10a).

Believers in Christ need to fellowship with other believers for worship, nurture, and encouragement. But they also need occasions when they are taught by each other. They need opportunities to test their own understandings of God's Word and will. We can study and learn alone but we should not attempt to understand the teachings of the Bible alone or to live the Christian life alone.

God wants us to live with a zeal to study, to learn, and to understand. But God also wants us to have the humility to test our interpretations of the Bible with others. After all, the Holy Spirit is revealing His truth to them as well as to us.

John R. W. Stott provides a fitting conclusion to this chapter and this section on insights for successful study.

The individual Christian's humble, prayerful, diligent, and obedient study of Scripture is not the only way the Holy Spirit makes clear what He has revealed. It would hardly be humble to ignore what the Spirit may have shown to others. The Holy Spirit is indeed our Teacher, but He teaches us indirectly through others as well as directly to our own minds. It was not to one man that He revealed the truths now enshrined in Scripture, but to a multiplicity of prophets and apostles; His work of illumination is given to many also.[2]

QUESTIONS FOR REFLECTION OR DISCUSSION

1. What examples have you seen of people misusing or abusing the Bible?

2. What difference have you experienced in Bible study since becoming a Christian?

3. What truth do you now know that you are hesitating to follow? What is holding you from obedience?

4. What passage of Scripture is unclear to you? Which principle of interpretation will help you find an answer to your question?

Notes

1. Carl F. H. Henry, ed., *Revelation and the Bible* (Philadelphia: Presbyterian and Reformed Publishing Company, 1958), p. 206.
2. John R. W. Stott, *Understanding the Bible* (Glendale, Calif.: Regal Books, 1973), p. 214.

PART II
METHODS OF SUCCESSFUL STUDY

5

Patterns of Bible Reading

Every person who has had personal acquaintance with the Bible has experienced *reading* the Bible. Of the many approaches to the Bible, reading is the most common. We will begin our examination of various methods of study with simple reading because all of us can identify with this approach.

Even though the approach of reading can be simple, it can also become extremely meaningful. Some of the world's outstanding Christians have followed this effective pattern. John Newton is one example. He said:

> I know not a better rule of reading the Scripture than to read it through from beginning to end; and when we have finished it once, to begin it again. We shall meet with many passages which we can make little improvement of; but not so many in the second reading as in the first; and fewer in the third than in the second.[1]

The Value of Bible Reading

John Newton identified one of the values of systematic reading; namely, increased understanding of the Bible's message. There is an important principle in Bible study. The more we know about the Bible the more we are able to benefit from reading it. The reverse also is true. The less we know about the Bible the less we seem to gain from our reading.

On the surface this appears to create an unsolvable problem. Young Christians who know little about the Bible often gain little from their reading and eventually become discouraged. This is why young Christians need help in what to read and how to read with profit. This is also why Bible study grows in its value to us as our Bible knowledge increases.

This fact leads to a second value in systematic Bible reading. It gives us an overview of the entire Bible. There is great value in being able to rise above the details of a given verse or chapter and to have an "aerial" view of the entire Scriptures.

When my wife and I moved to the Washington, D.C., area, I found the city very confusing. One Saturday I needed to make pastoral calls in several hospitals. I needed to check the map numerous times as the avenue I was following would suddenly become a street with a different name or a street would become an avenue. After the frustration of this experience, I spent some time studying a map of the city. Soon afterwards I went to the top of Washington's monument so I could get an overview of the nation's capital.

I looked down on Washington and saw the systematic pattern dividing the city into four sections. I observed the way in which North, East and South Capitol streets go out from the Capitol building like giant spokes from the hub of a wheel. I observed the pattern of numbered and lettered streets and the angling avenues. Finally, I saw that the city was actually very orderly and that understanding its pattern would make it possible to know exactly where I was even though the streets were strange. This was an important discovery that made driving easy and the map almost unnecessary.

Similarly a disciplined pattern of Bible reading acquaints the reader with the major sections of the Bible. You marvel at the beginnings of the universe, of man, and of the people of God. You are amazed at the pioneering of the Patriarchs. You ache with the despair and folly of the Judges. You sense the excitement and the glory of the Kings. You stand in silence listening to the thunder of the Prophets. Your heart is warmed with the compassionate ministry of Jesus. You examine your own life as you ponder the instructions of the Epistles. And your eyes are raised from earth to heaven as you reflect on the coming Lord of glory whose Revelation we await.

Is it any wonder that some Christians choose to read through the Bible again and again?

George Muller of Bristol was one of these persons. He read through the Bible 100 times and knew it so well he was ashamed if he needed to resort to a concordance. Here is his own testimony:

> The vigor of our Spiritual Life will be in exact proportion to the place held by the Bible in our life and thoughts. I solemnly state this from the experience of fifty-four years.
>
> The first three years after conversion I neglected the Word of God. Since I began to search it diligently the blessing has been wonderful.
>
> I have read the Bible through one hundred times, and always with increasing delight. Each time it seems like a new book to me.
>
> Great has been the blessing from consecutive, diligent, daily study. I look upon it as a lost day when I have not had a good time over the Word of God.[2]

Dr. Harry Ironsides is reported to have read the Bible through 72 times by the time he was 72 years of age. Eventually he became blind but continued preaching because he knew the Bible so well.

The Possibility of Reading Through the Bible

Read the Bible through 72 times or 100 times? That sounds impossible, doesn't it? But what about *one* time? Does that sound possible? I once had a professor who said that the average reader could read through the Bible in 60 hours. I considered myself an average reader and was sure that it would take me much longer than that. So to prove that the professor was wrong, I tried it. Indeed he was wrong. To my surprise it took only 57 hours and 45 minutes! I read slowly enough to ponder certain verses and underline others. I was really amazed. So it is possible to read through the entire Bible.

There are various systematic ways suggested to help in this venture. The most common is to read a certain number of chapters each day so as to complete the reading in one year. Remember that there are 1,189 chapters in the Bible.

One pattern is to read three chapters a day and five on Sunday.

Another pattern is to read one chapter from the New Testament each day except Sunday, and to read two chapters from the Old Testament each day except Sunday. On Sunday read five chapters from the Old Testament. This pattern has the advantage of keeping the reader related to both the more familiar New Testament and the less familiar Old Testament at the same time.

Still another pattern is to read a certain number of pages each day. Take your Bible and divide 365 into the total number of pages. Most Bibles will require reading three or four pages a day to complete the reading in one year.

It should be kept in mind that the objective is not to simply read the Bible through. Rather, the objective is to expose ourselves to the Scriptures so that we better understand God's message and so that He can speak to us. It is much better to read primarily in the New Testament or Psalms, than to begin in Genesis and give up in despair about the middle of Leviticus.

Suppose you decide to read through the Bible. How will you read? What approach will you follow? I have observed and experienced three primary patterns of Bible reading.

Casual Reading

Casual reading is reading without a particular purpose in mind. If some verse or truth speaks to you, that is all right. If nothing stands out as you read, that is all right too. If you remember something you read, fine. If not, that also is fine.

How well I remember my earliest attempt to read through the Bible. My Sunday school teacher had given each pupil a leaflet that listed all of the books of the Bible. Beside each book was a small block for each chapter. As chapters were read, it was a great delight to fill in the blocks with a red pencil. I especially liked the Psalms because the chapters were short and it took less time to read the three chapters each day and fill in the blocks!

Obviously my purpose in reading was to fill in the chapter blocks and hopefully complete the project so that I could prove I had read the entire Bible.

Needless to say, I was a casual reader. The Scriptures seldom spoke to me and I didn't mind. I seldom remembered what I had read and that was all right too. Unfortunately, I felt comfortable with this casual approach.

I was reading the Bible with the same attitude as many

Sunday afternoon drivers. They are out driving but not going any place in particular and not looking for anything special. They are simply driving. That is all that matters. I was simply reading and that was all that concerned me.

Casual reading may be better than no reading—I was getting some exposure to the Bible—but there are much better approaches that can be followed.

Reflective Reading

To read reflectively is to read with your mind alert and your eyes open to some new discovery. It is to approach the Bible with a hunger to be fed and an anticipation of finding some fresh truth. It is to read with the prayer of Samuel, "Speak, Lord, for your servant is listening" (1 Samuel 3:9).

To use the Sunday afternoon driver illustration again, it is like taking a drive for the purpose of seeing some new and interesting sight.

Several years ago I took my elderly mother for a Sunday afternoon drive through the country to see the fall scenery. She constantly remarked about some new house she had not seen before or some especially colorful tree. We were driving just to see what we could see and we saw many new things. We were driving reflectively.

Oswald J. Smith is a good example of a person who practiced reflective reading. In an article entitled "The Morning Watch," he described the way he read his Bible.

> For over forty years now I have observed the Morning Watch. I commence by reading the Word of God, remembering the words, "As newborn babes, desire the sincere milk of the word, that ye may grow thereby" (1 Peter 2:2). Then in obedience to Psalm 5:3, "My voice shalt thou hear in the morning, O Lord; in the morning will I direct my prayer unto thee, and will look up," I turn to prayer.

When I was saved I was asked for my Bible by a personal worker, who wrote on the flyleaf, "This Book will keep you from sin, or sin will keep you from this Book." And I have found it to be true. The two cannot go together.

I always use the . . . Bible and I have one of the largest published. I mark it and as I grow older and find it more difficult to read, I am grateful for the large type.

The reason so many do not enjoy the Bible is because they do not know the Author. It is one thing to meet Jesus Christ at the time of conversion; it is quite another to become acquainted with Him by spending time in His presence.

The Bible should be read daily just as the manna was gathered daily. We would not dream of taking only one meal a day, much less a week, since our bodies need to be nourished. Yet some of us, I am afraid, neglect the spiritual good that is even more essential. I have read the Word of God for over forty years, 365 days in the year, and I expect to read it every day until I see my Lord face-to-face.

I read the Word of God as I would read a letter, or as I would eat fish. When I get a letter I start at the beginning and read to the end. That is the way to study the Word. Start with the first chapter of Genesis and read to the last word of Revelation, reading two or three chapters a day, and then do it again. I do not know how many times I have read the Bible through. If I come to a verse that I cannot understand, I do not cast the book aside any more than I would throw away my plate of fish because of a bone. I simply lay it aside and go on reading, as I would go on eating. Then when I read it again, some of the statements that I thought were bones I am able to digest.

When you read God's Word He talks to you. When you pray you talk to Him. After a time with the Book, I turn to prayer and thus I become acquainted with the Lord Jesus Christ.[3]

Another example of reflective reading is the pattern followed by Mary Slessor of Calabar, an early missionary to Africa. Her focus was on mastering a book at a time and eventually covering the entire Bible.

She would read early in the morning beginning at day break. Slowly and carefully she would read through a

chapter underlining key words and sentences. The objective
was to discover the intended meaning of the author. Sometimes she would spend the study time of two or three days
with a given chapter because she would not leave it until she
was certain of its central purpose and message. In the
margins, she would note new truths, fresh lessons, and other
insights. When the study of one Bible was completed, she
would take a new Bible and repeat the process. This approach provided a freshness in Bible reading year after year.
She harvested the fruit of reflective reading.

Research Reading

The pattern of Mary Slessor suggests a third approach to
reading; namely, research reading. In this approach, you
read the Bible looking for a specific teaching and record
your findings. As a scientist does research in his laboratory,
collecting and recording data, so the Bible student gathers
information and records his findings. Referring once more to
the Sunday afternoon driver, it is like persons building a
house, who go for a drive to look at new houses for help in
discovering current color schemes of brick, shingles, and
paint. By carefully examining other houses, they decide the
selection of colors they will use for their house. This is research driving.

Everek R. Storms, an active church worker from
Kitchener, Ontario, followed the pattern of reading through
the Bible and doing research on a particular subject. During
one of the readings, he listed the promises mentioned in the
Bible. Mr. Storms had always questioned the statement that
there are 30,000 promises in the Scriptures so he decided to
check for himself. He found that there are 8,810 promises
recorded. An article about Mr. Storms catagorized the
promises as follows:

> 7,487 promises God has given to mankind, 991 where one man makes promises to another man, 290 promises made by man to God, and 28 promises made by angels. He also found nine "promises" which were made by Satan.[4]

Research reading requires some effort and discipline but it is both exciting and rewarding. It requires a Bible, paper, pencil, and the willingness to record what you find, but you are rewarded by lasting benefits.

When *The Exorcist* was shown in theaters across the nation, the subject of demons and exorcism became a contemporary topic for discussion. Some believed in demons; some did not. Some promoted exorcism and others opposed it.

I became curious about the New Testament's teaching on these subjects, so I did some research reading. I read through the New Testament looking for references to Satan, demons and exorcism, and angels. The findings were recorded on sheets of paper with a column for each of the three subjects. After the research project was finished, it was easy to see at a glance which books of the New Testament gave special attention to these topics.

For example, I discovered that Matthew has much to say about demons and exorcism, and angels. Mark has a lot to say about demons and exorcism but almost no reference to angels. John has few references to either demons or angels.

By contrast, some of the later New Testament books such as 1 and 2 Thessalonians, 1 and 2 Timothy, 1 Peter, and 1 John have much to say about Satan, but very little to say about demons or angels. Revelation, on the other hand, has many references to angels and also frequent references to Satan.

I concluded therefore that not all books of the New Testament give equal attention to these doctrines. The New Testament writers did not have a "demon fixation."

However, the existence of supernatural beings in our universe is overwhelmingly affirmed and these beings are agents for both good and evil. It is also clear that Christ alone is the One who triumphs over all evil, whether the evil ones be men, demons, or Satan. Therefore, united with the Victor, we are certain of victory even though we experience spiritual conflict. In fact, a central theme of the New Testament is Christ's victory over every form of sin, rebellion, and ungodliness. How thrilling! How reassuring to keep this truth in mind in our godless age.

Recently I have been pondering two areas of concern. First, what does it mean for God to bless His followers? If you listen to some radio and TV preachers, you are told that contributing to their programs will result in God blessing you in a special way. This special blessing will be financial. God will multiply your dollars as Christ multiplied the loaves and fishes. They imply that the surest way to riches is through giving generously to their causes.

Does the Bible really support this position? Does this position confuse God's promises in the Old Testament and the New Testament? Does God promise financial success to all of His faithful children throughout the New Testament age? If so, why are so many believers in other parts of the world in poverty?

A second and related question is, how does God really expect wealthy Christians to help the poor in our society? Some say that Christians should not accumulate wealth in the first place because they should constantly be sharing their abundance with the poor. Others say that wealth is alright if gotten honestly and that spiritual poverty, rather than material poverty, should be our concern. If you are busy in personal evangelism, you don't need to be concerned about the hungry and the underprivileged. What light does the Bible throw on these questions? How would Christ answer them if He were here in His body of flesh today?

So, I have begun another research reading project. Presently I am reading through the Bible and recording references relating to these important questions. After completing the research reading, I plan to give special study to the key passages and arrive at a biblical conclusion.

Research reading does require time, thought, and diligence. But this is precisely why it has significant rewards. I recommend it to you.

QUESTIONS FOR REFLECTION OR DISCUSSION

1. To what extent have you gained an overview of the Scriptures? What has been most helpful in achieving this overview?

2. If you have read through the Bible, what pattern did you follow? Would you recommend that pattern to others or do you have a better plan to suggest?

3. Of the three primary patterns of Bible reading described, which ones have you experienced? What new insights did you receive?

4. What questions have you been considering which could be explored through a research reading of the Scriptures?

Notes

1. Evans, op. cit., p. 137.
2. Henry H. Halley, *Pocket Bible Handbook* (Chicago: Henry H. Halley, 1951) p. 5.
3. Oswald J. Smith, "The Morning Watch," *The Christian Ministry*, October-December, 1957, pp. 182, 183.
4. C. J. Rempel, "Reads Entire Bible 27 Times," *Mennonite Weekly Review*, December 20, 1956, p. 9.

6

Methods of Bible Meditation

How often we have heard the statement, "Christians have lost the art of meditation." Meditation is a little like the weather. Many people talk about it but few do anything about it!

The practice of meditation has been a part of man's religious experience since the dawn of history. When Isaac was anxiously waiting for his father's servant to bring him a wife, he went out to meditate in the field. Today a person in a similar situation would likely spend the time "pacing the floor" or "climbing the walls," instead of meditating!

The practice of meditation in the Old Testament seems to have reached its peak during the time of King David. When you read the Psalms the idea and reality of meditation becomes very alive. In fact, for the psalmist, the question was not, do you meditate? Rather, the question was, on what do you meditate? This may be the best question for us also.

The psalmist lived with the prayer, "May the words of my mouth and the meditation of my heart be pleasing in your sight, O Lord, my Rock and my Redeemer" (Psalm 19:14). His prayer was practiced in life. Psalm 119 has many references to the Word of God and meditation. Here are a few examples:

> I reach out my hands for your
>   commandments, which I love,
>   and I meditate on your decrees (verse 48).
>
> Oh, how I love your law!
>   I meditate on it all day long (verse 97).
>
> My eyes stay open through the
>   watches of the night,
>   that I may meditate on your
>   promises (verse 148).

The psalmist was carrying out the instructions God had earlier given to Israel. After the death of Moses, God chose Joshua to become Israel's leader. A part of his assignment related to meditation. "Do not let this Book of the Law depart from your mouth; meditate on it day and night, so that you may be careful to do everything written in it. Then you will be prosperous and successful" (Joshua 1:8).

Today the concept and practice of meditation is being revived. Eastern religions are promoting the practice through yoga and transcendental meditation. At the same time numerous Christian authors are calling believers back to the biblical pattern and practice of meditation.

Why? Because our inner lives are shallow and empty. We feed our minds with facts and our bodies with food but our spirits or souls are either starved or malnourished. We have learned religious phrases but we lack religious reality. We can talk about God but we seldom talk to God. Our relationship with God is more nearly that of a distant relative than an intimate companion as described by the psalmist.

But, you ask, what is meditation and why is it so important? In the last chapter, we described Bible reading. Here the emphasis was on exposure to a rather lengthy portion of Scripture, perhaps three chapters or three pages at a time. In meditation the emphasis is focusing on a smaller passage and reading more leisurely. The primary purpose is to gain spiritual strength and personal spiritual blessings. The central concern is finding spiritual food that will enrich your life today. In meditation, you read with the question, what truth does God have in this passage for me?

Andrew Murray, a man who knew well the art and reward of meditation, described it in the following way:

> It is in meditation that the heart holds and appropriates the Word. Just as in reflection the understanding grasps all the meaning of a truth, so in meditation the heart assimilates it and makes it a part of its own life. We need continual reminding that the heart means the will and the affection. The meditation of the heart implies desires, acceptance, surrender, love. What the heart truly believes, that it receives with love and joy, and allows to master and rule the life. The intellect gathers and prepares the food upon which we are to feed. In meditation the heart takes it in and feeds on it.[1]

In meditation we treat a biblical truth the way we treated an all-day sucker when we were children or the way we eat hard Christmas candy. We let the candy slowly dissolve in our mouths so that the taste can be enjoyed for a prolonged period of time and we can get the maximum benefit. We never experience the potential delight if we give the candy a quick chew and a swallow!

Behind the experience of meditation there must be a quiet, meditative spirit. The psalmist expressed this spirit when he wrote, "Be still, and know that I am God" (Psalm 46:10). The prophet Isaiah declared a similar message when he said, "In quietness and trust is your strength" (Isaiah 30:15).

Merrill C. Tenney described the meditative spirit when he stated:

> Devotional study is not so much a technique as a spirit. It is the spirit of eagerness which seeks the mind of God; it is the spirit of humility which listens readily to the voice of God; it is the spirit of adventure which pursues earnestly the will of God; it is the spirit of adoration which rests in the presence of God.[2]

Ellen Riley recommended combining silence with meditation. Her pattern was to read a passage of Scripture to cleanse and fill her mind. Then she would sit with God in silence. Within several years, the daily time in silence grew from four minutes to over an hour.

In addition to a meditative spirit, there must be a proper attitude toward the Scriptures. Some Christians have a host of nagging questions about the Bible. Is the Bible simply a religious book similar to the most important writings of other religions? Is its level of inspiration the same as the writings of contemporary Christian authors? Or does the Bible uniquely reveal the mind and will of God? Will God really speak to me through the pages of Scripture?

We will not be motivated to meditate, listening for a word from God unless we accept the Bible as the Word of God. John R. W. Stott expressed this fact quite clearly:

> Do we really believe that *God* has spoken, that *God's* words are recorded in Scripture, and that as we read it we may hear *God's* voice addressing us? Then we shall not grudge the time to listen. Instead, we shall want to register our protest against the rat-race of twentieth-century life and strive to recover the lost art of meditation. It is not a casual, superficial acquaintance with Scripture that the modern church needs, but rather to heed our Master's exhortation: "Let these words sink into your ears."[3] There is no particular secret about how to do it. It just takes time, purposefully

redeemed from our busy lives, in which to turn Scripture over and over in our minds until it sinks into our hearts and so regulates everything we think and do.[4]

We should not forget that the purpose of biblical meditation is to encounter the living God as revealed in our Lord Jesus Christ. To hear Him speak is an unparalleled privilege and provides untold blessings. And while our major concern is message rather than method, there are certain methods that aid in receiving God's message. Methods that distract from message are a hindrance and should be discarded. I have experienced some of these and perhaps you have too. But I have also experienced several methods that have enhanced my hearing God's message. I will share these approaches with you and encourage you to try them. New approaches may result in new messages.

Dialoguing with God

John Baillie told about his conversation with a man who came to him after he had preached in a university chapel. As they walked together, the stranger expressed the feelings of many Christians.

> "You speak," he said, "of trusting God, of praying to Him and doing His will. But *it's all so one-sided.* We speak to God, we bow down before Him and lift up our hearts to Him. But He never speaks to us. He makes no sign. *It's all so one-sided.*"

Yes, it can be "all so one-sided." And that one side can be man's side or God's side. We may worship and pray and praise without hearing God speak. Or God may speak continually and repeatedly through His Word and we fail to respond. Either way the communication is incomplete.

What we desire is conversation, not mere contemplation; dialogue, not monologue.

One way to experience dialoguing with God is by responding to His Word to us as recorded in the Scriptures. Or as John Stott expressed it, as we read the Scriptures, we may hear God's voice addressing us. How then should we respond?

Dialoguing with God through the Scriptures is simply reading a small passage and responding to God by talking to Him about what He has said to us. It is reflecting back to God what is going through our minds. The response may be thanksgiving, praise, questions, repentance, or any other response that expresses what we would say to God if He were speaking to us in a visible, physical form.

For this type of meditation or spiritual exercise, we should have privacy because we simply want to dialogue with God, not talk to man about God.

Not all passages lend themselves to this type of meditation. However, it is effective with the Psalms, the Gospels, and the Epistles.

In a college course in the devotional life, I asked the students to dialogue with God as they responded to an assigned passage. Notice the response moving from questions, to confession, to petitions, to praise. The passage was James 3:13-18.

> Who is wise and understanding among you? By his good life let him show his works in the meekness of wisdom. But if you have bitter jealousy and selfish ambition in your hearts, do not boast and be false to the truth. This wisdom is not such as comes down from above, but is earthly, unspiritual, devilish. For where jealousy and selfish ambition exist, there will be disorder and every vile practice. But the wisdom from above is first pure, then peaceable, gentle, open to reason, full of mercy and good fruits, without uncertainty or

insincerity. And the harvest of righteousness is sown in peace by those who make peace (RSV).

One student responded in a very personal way.

> Lord, what is meekness of wisdom? Father I know I shouldn't have bitter jealousy and selfish ambition in my heart and I shouldn't boast. Help me to be more honest and open to Your love that can surpass my human nature. Yes, Lord, I have experienced this earthly, unspiritual, devilish wisdom but I too have experienced Your wisdom which is pure, peaceable, gentle, open to reason, full of mercy and good fruits, without uncertainty and insincerity and I know that Yours is much better and rewarding. Help me to desire this kind of wisdom. Help me to be a person of peace, Lord, and therefore a reaper of righteousness. Thank you, Lord, for speaking to me today through Your Word.

Recently I was meditating on 1 John 5:13. "I write these things to you who believe in the name of the Son of God so that you may know that you have eternal life." My dialogue with God went something like this.

> Lord, that's really great. I believe in the name of the Son of God. I believe in Jesus as Your only Son. So, Lord, You have written these words to me. And not only to me but to all the people who believe. And, Lord, You want me and all others who believe to *know* that we have eternal life.
>
> What does it mean to know, Lord? Does it mean to know like I know my name—something I have learned? Or does it mean to know like I know I'm married—something I've experienced? Or could it be both kinds of knowing? Likely.
>
> Thanks, Lord, that I do know You in this double way. I was taught about You and I have experienced Your presence, Your pardon, Your peace. Thanks so much, Lord.
>
> But You want me to know that I have eternal life in this deep way of knowing. Eternal life—a special kind of life that will not end when I die, Your kind of life.
>
> Lord, I do want to know that I have this kind of life. I say that I know but I can't really understand it. Eternal life!
>
> Lord, teach me, teach me, teach me. . . .

Now it is your turn. Select a passage and as you read, respond to God's message to you. You will be dialoguing with God. Your spirit will be refreshed.

Retuning Relationships

A second method of meditation is to reflect on a passage of Scripture to see what it teaches about life's various relationships.

Jesus said that the greatest commandment is to "love the Lord your God with all your heart and with all your soul and with all your mind and with all your strength." The second greatest commandment is to "love your neighbor as yourself" (Mark 12:30, 31). He is saying that the heart of the Christian life is a new, loving relationship with God and man. We can expect the Word of God to tell us about the kinds of relationships God wants us to have and to show us where our relationships need to be retuned.

The total Bible message can be understood as an account of the relationship between God and mankind. At the dawn of creation, Adam and Eve lived in the Garden of Eden in perfect harmony with God and each other. Their sin destroyed their harmonious living and their relationship changed to conflict and separation.

The sacrifices and laws of the Old Testament were to help restore these relationships. They failed because of human weakness. Christ came to restore mankind to God and to each other. This new quality of life should be experienced now in the church. Perfect harmony will again be ours when Christ returns and we live with Him in the new heaven and new earth. Until that time, the Bible is our guide to godly living which means following God's plan for all of life's relationships. We meditate on the Scriptures to learn what relationships need to be strengthened, corrected, or retuned.

God is concerned with our relationships in at least four main areas. He is concerned about our relationship to Him, to ourselves, to other believers, and to society or the world. The diagram below attempts to illustrate the way in which we are related to these four areas.

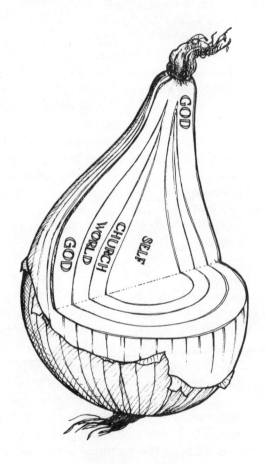

Diagram by James A. Harris

We are at the center of our own world. Try as we may we cannot get away from ourselves. The Scriptures have much to say about how individuals should relate to themselves. When Jesus said that we should love our neighbor as ourselves, He implied that we should have a proper respect for ourselves because we are made in the image of God, even as we respect and love our neighbor. God does not teach self-hatred.

A second important relationship is with God. Through faith in His Son Jesus, we can have a living union with Him. Paul highlighted this relationship when he said that "in him we live and move and have our being" (Acts 17:28). Repeatedly the Scriptures tell us about the total love we are to have for God.

A third area of relationships is with our fellow Christians. When we are united to Christ, we become united to all others in the body of Christ, the church. Other believers are our brothers and sisters even though we do not know them. We are to relate to those that we do know with love, compassion, and honesty. The Scriptures contain many instructions about our relationships in this area.

The fourth major area to which we are constantly related is the world or society. In Jesus' High Priestly Prayer, He said, "My prayer is not that you take them out of the world but that you protect them from the evil one" (John 17:15). Since this is a concern of Jesus, the Bible tells us what our relationship to the world should be and what it should not be.

A valuable exercise is to take a paragraph or larger passage of Scripture and to meditate on what it teaches about each of these relationships. I suggest that you experience meditation with a focus on retuning your relationships. Take your Bible and read 1 John 2:1-17. As you read, look for teachings that speak to your relationships to self, God, church, and world. As you identify the teachings, ask yourself what the teachings mean and whether any of your relationships need to be retuned. Turn to 1 John 2 and try this experiment.

What did you find as you read? You likely observed that verse 4 deals with our being honest with ourselves about our spiritual lives. Verses 5 and 6 touch on our relationship with God and our following Christ as our example in life. Verses 9 to 11 speak powerfully about our relationships with our brothers and sisters in Christ. Finally, verses 15 to 17 speak pointedly about our relationship to the world.

In meditating on these relationships, we reflect on God's teachings and our own lives. We prayerfully ask what relationships need to be changed to bring our lives into harmony with His plan and pattern. Of course, most passages of Scripture do not speak to all four relationships of life but most passages do speak of at least one of these relationships. Therefore, most passages help us retune our lives.

Comprehending Content

A third method of meditation is to examine a passage for its basic content. Much of the Bible contains important truths that God wants us to know and understand. These truths become the foundation of our Christian beliefs and actions. Without them our faith has no foundation and our lives have no direction.

Most passages of Scripture contain either basic doctrines, general instructions, or personal promises. As we reflect on these types of teachings, we discover that doctrines are to be believed, instructions are to be followed, and promises are to be claimed. These actions are at the heart of the Christian life—believing, following, claiming.

Doctrines to believe include the major beliefs of the

Christian faith. This could include what the Bible teaches about God, Jesus Christ, the Holy Spirit, man, angels, Satan, temptation, prayer, repentance, conversion, the Scriptures, marriage, and many other areas of teaching. God wants us to grow in our knowledge of Him. This takes place when we discover the doctrinal teachings of the Bible and believe them as God's eternal truth.

In the Christian life, knowledge precedes experience. People do not become Christians or experience the new birth until they know about the death and resurrection of Jesus. These teachings are doctrines of the Bible. When we know about them and believe them as truth, then God makes us new persons in Christ. Doctrines are to be believed.

Instructions to follow include the numerous teachings revealing how God wants us to live. There are some specific commands that we are to obey. The Ten Commandments would be an example. There are various lists of sins that we are to avoid. These lists include sins of thought, word, and deed. Then there are attitudes to reflect and attitudes to reject. Also, there are examples of persons to follow and to refrain from following. The Apostle Paul says that the Old Testament stories are for our instruction.

The Christian is a disciple, a follower of Christ. We should therefore read the Bible looking for Christ's words of instruction to us. Instructions are to be followed.

Promises to claim are found throughout the Scriptures. We noticed in chapter 5 that there are 7,487 promises that God has given to mankind. Obviously some of these were directed to specific persons in specific situations and are not applicable to all believers. God promised a son to Abraham and Sarah when he was 100 and she was 90 years old. The promise was difficult for them to understand and believe but

God kept His promise and Isaac was born. God did not intend this promise for all couples the ages of Abraham and Sarah. It was given to them and them alone.

Catherine Marshall helps us understand promises when she identifies those that begin with *whoever.* Many of God's promises are for all of God's people. These are the whoever promises. A familiar example is John 3:16. "For God so loved the world that he gave his one and only Son, that whoever believes in him shall not perish but have eternal life."

We should keep in mind that many of God's promises are for all people even though the word *whoever* is not used. Reading the context usually shows us whether a particular promise is one we are to claim or was intended for one particular person. And remember that a promise must be claimed to be experienced.

On one occasion, I was facing a situation that caused me to be worried and anxious. Somewhat accidently, I started to read chapter 4 of Philippians. Suddenly I was jolted by what I read.

> Do not be anxious about anything, but in everything, by prayer and petition, with thanksgiving, present your requests to God. And the peace of God, which transcends all understanding, will guard your hearts and your minds in Christ Jesus.   —*Philippians 4:6, 7*

"God," I asked, "can this be true? Can You give me a peace that transcends my understanding?" After prayerful reflection, the Holy Spirit assured me it could be true. This promise is for me. It is for all of God's children. In a step of faith, I claimed the promise. God was faithful to His promise. He gave me an inner peace beyond my ability to describe. It was the "peace of God."

I like the way Catherine Marshall describes the claiming process.

> God has made a promise
>
> If there are conditions attached to it, we do our best to meet them.
>
> We make an act of claiming this promise at a specific time and place.
>
> God fulfills the promise in His own time and His own way.[6]

It is now your turn to comprehend content. Turn to 1 John 2:18-25. As you meditate on this passage, look for doctrines to believe, instructions to follow, and promises to claim. Then finish reading this chapter.

What did you discover? You likely discovered that verses 18 and 19 refer to the doctrine of the Antichrist and Antichrists (those that are against Christ). Verses 20 to 24 instruct us to continue in our belief that Jesus is the Christ. If we deny this belief we become an Antichrist. Verses 24 and 25 present a promise. If we continue to believe that Jesus is divine, God promises us eternal life.

This passage contains the three areas of content. Obviously, this is not the case of all passages but most passages will include at least one of the three.

Within each of us is a desire to become strong in faith, to be a mature Christian. This will happen if we continue a life of Bible meditation and study. The testimony of D. L. Moody can become the testimony of every Christian.

> I prayed for Faith, and thought that some day Faith would come down and strike me like lightning. But Faith did not seem to come.
>
> One day I read in the tenth chapter of Romans, "Now Faith cometh by hearing, and hearing by the Word of God."

I had closed my Bible, and prayed for Faith. I now opened my Bible, and began to study, and Faith has been growing ever since.[7]

QUESTIONS FOR REFLECTION OR DISCUSSION

1. Try to recall a time in your life when you experienced meaningful meditation. What made it so meaningful?

2. How would you evaluate your attempt at dialoguing with God? Fair? Good? Great? What did you learn through the experience?

3. As you examined your own relationships in light of the teachings in 1 John 2:1-17, what needy areas came to your mind? What have you done to retune these relationships?

4. Reflect on specific promises in the Bible that you have claimed. Which ones caused major changes in your life? Which ones do you hesitate to claim?

Notes

1. Wilbur M. Smith, *Profitable Bible Study* (Boston: W. A. Wilde Co., 1953), p. 63.
2. Merrill C. Tenney, *Galatians: The Charter of Christian Liberty* (Grand Rapids: Eerdmans, 1954), pp. 189, 190.
3. Luke 9:44.
4. Stott, op. cit., p. 243.
5. John Baillie, *The Idea of Revelation in Recent Thought* (New York: Columbia University Press, 1956), p. 137.
6. Catherine Marshall, *Adventures in Prayer* (Old Tappan, N.J.: Spire Books, 1975), pp. 107, 108.
7. Halley, op. cit., p. 5.

Tips on Memorization

Imagine one of your friends asking you to join in a regular plan of Bible memorization. How would you respond? Would you reply positively or negatively? Your response might be, "I can't memorize. I don't have the time." Or you might respond, "I really would like to give it a try."

You Can Memorize

Many adults can recall verses they memorized in Sunday school when they were children. It seemed easy at that age but now they feel it is no longer possible. It may be that the speed of memorization is slower for the adult but studies indicate that those who could memorize as a child can still memorize as an adult.

Some persons who have memorized a large number of Scripture verses started the process in middle age or older. Henry H. Halley began memorizing when he was 39 years old. In spite of his claim of having an ordinary memory, he memorized nearly one fourth of the Bible. Of course it took time—two to three hours a day for ten years. But in the process, his life was greatly enriched and his knowledge of the Bible was radically increased.

There was also a person who began memorizing after the age of sixty. In time he memorized the Gospel of John, Romans, the Sermon on the Mount, fifty psalms, plus other passages. He too experienced life-changing effects.

Most persons who memorize the Scriptures gain personal values that enrich their lives. What are these values?

The Scriptures Are Immediately Available

We live in an age of computers. In the recent past, most businesses have computerized their operations. Why? One major reason is the possibility and value of an immediate re-call of information. Data concerning accounts, inventory, and sales is fed into an electronic brain. By simply pushing the right buttons the information is flashed onto a screen or typed on a printout. What an asset to the business!

The human mind is similar to a computer. We memorize information and store it in our brains. When the right "button" is pushed, that information is flashed onto the screens of our consciousness. What an asset to our lives!

Scriptures that are memorized have special value to us because they are immediately available. At a moment's notice, we can think through them in our minds or share them with our tongues.

As a young Christian, I had an urge to witness but was paralyzed by a fear related to my ignorance of the Bible. As my knowledge of the Bible increased through memorization of selected Scriptures, the fear began to leave and witnessing increased.

The Apostle Peter must have known about the value of memorization for witnessing, because he gave the following instructions: "Always be prepared to give an answer to everyone who asks you to give the reason for the hope that you have" (1 Peter 3:15b).

Having the Scriptures in your mind for immediate recall is also valuable when faced with temptation. Jesus faced His temptation by Satan with the reply, "It is written." He then quoted passages from Deuteronomy and Psalms that related specifically to the particular temptation. Apparently Jesus had these passages in His mind for immediate recall.

The Scriptures Are More Easily Understood

A valuable exercise is to reflect on both familiar and puzzling passages that you have memorized. In the process, familiar passages take on new meaning through fresh insights and puzzling passages grow in value as their mystery is replaced with understanding.

Recently while mowing the lawn, I was reflecting on the Beatitudes. I was attempting to understand more clearly what Jesus meant when He said, "Blessed are those who are persecuted because of righteousness, for theirs is the kingdom of heaven" (Matthew 5:10). While thinking through all of the Beatitudes (verses 3 to 12), I discovered that the beatitude preceding the one on persecution, focuses on peacemaking. It says, "Blessed are the peacemakers, for they will be called the sons of God" (Matthew 5:9).

I recalled that in the Bible, the word for peace means wholeness of life or total well-being. Jesus pronounces a blessing on those who make peace, who attempt to bring wholeness to the lives of others. But this is immediately followed by a reference to persecution.

New understanding was beginning to unfold. As the Christian witnesses to bring peace to those who are in conflict, the efforts are often misunderstood by one or both parties in the conflict, and the result is hostility toward the peacemaker. The peacemaker may experience rejection and persecution for righteousness' sake. Or as the Christian works to bring wholeness to those who are deprived and oppressed, the oppressors may become hostile toward the peacemaker. Persecution may be the result. After all, isn't this what Jesus experienced? Isn't this what many since Jesus' day have also experienced? I finished mowing the lawn, refreshed by a new understanding of the Scriptures I had memorized.

The Scriptures Can Be Used in New Ways

Scriptures that are memorized have many new uses. When our oldest child was in the lower grades of Sunday school, the pupils were asked to memorize various passages of Scripture. The memorizing was to be done at home and each pupil would then recite the passage in class.

As my wife and I talked about the assignment and the help we could give him in memorizing, we decided to try a new and painless approach. We would use the assigned passage as our family prayer at breakfast. By "praying over" the passage each day, we would be learning it without special effort. It could be a family project, not simply an assignment for him.

My wife typed the passage and hung it near the table. Each morning we read it as our prayer. Gradually the passage became so familiar we could pray it with our eyes closed. We had memorized a passage with little effort.

By that time, the passage had become rich with meaning, so we simply continued using it as a family prayer. Eventually we memorized various passages such as Psalm 23, Psalm 100, The Lord's Prayer, a part of John 14, and a part of 1 Corinthians 13. We are amazed how easily the younger children memorized the same passages, and therefore knew them before the assignment was given to them in their Sunday school classes.

The Sermon on the Mount, Matthew 5—7, has been a favorite part of the Bible for a number of years. Soon after I was ordained to the ministry, I memorized these chapters, believing they would enrich my life. During the memorizing process, I became aware of the power of the Scriptures. I became aware of the penetrating way Jesus stated truth. His sermon was so much better than any I prepared that I decided to share the Sermon on the Mount from memory on a Sunday morning. The passage spoke in a new way to the congregation because the Scriptures were being used in a new way.

The Scriptures Cannot Be Taken from Us

What we have in our minds belongs to us and cannot be taken from us. We often say that our thoughts are our own. This is true because they are hidden from others, but it is also true because others cannot control our thoughts. Our possessions can be stolen and our bodies can be bound, but our knowledge cannot be bound or stolen.

I have heard people in prison say they are free. Why? Because their minds were filled with forgiveness, love, and hope. Their bodies were locked behind bars but their minds were free to dream dreams and think constructive thoughts.

I have also heard people who possessed little, say that they are rich. Why? Because their minds were filled with knowledge and experiences that could not be valued in dollars. All of this was theirs to keep.

Since the time of Christ, many people have lived without a Bible. There were times when Christians were locked in prison, away from the Bible. At other times the Bible was taken away from Christians and the copies destroyed. Out of

these situations have come many stories of individuals memorizing lengthy passages of Scripture which they then shared
with each other when they met to worship. The Bible could
be taken from their hands but not from their minds.

The list of values that come from memorizing Scriptures
could be enlarged. Few would deny that memorization is
valuable. But it should be remembered that the mere act of
committing Scriptures to memory does not automatically
bring spiritual benefits. Recently a man told me about his
father who is an atheist. He says that God does not exist and
makes light of his son who has become a believer. According
to the son, his father has "memorized the Bible" so that he
can argue with Christians. He has learned the words of the
Bible but has not responded to its message.

Ever since the Old Testament period, there have been
those who knew the Scriptures but who failed to respond to
its truths. The Jews told the story of a man who informed his
rabbi that he had read through the Talmud (Jewish commentaries on the law) three times. To this boast the rabbi replied: "The important thing is not how many times *you*
have been *through* the Talmud, but whether the Talmud
has been *through you!*"

I believe that most Christians really would like to
experience the values of memorizing Scriptures. They really
would like to have the Scriptures go through them—through
their minds, hearts, and lives. How then should they
proceed? What steps should they take?

Select the Best Translation

During the past 15 to 20 years, there has been a decline of
interest in memorizing Bible passages. There are many
reasons such as less encouragement from our Sunday schools
and more TV viewing to occupy our time. But I believe

another reason is the presence of many new translations. If you do decide to start memorizing, you still need to decide which translation to use.

This is the way some people may reason:

> I don't really know which translation to use for memorizing. The King James Version is the most familiar but some of its words are not clear. If I try to memorize it, I get lost. I have a few newer translations that are easier to read, but when I try memorizing from them, I get several different translations confused. So I'll give up my dream of memorizing.

How tragic! How happy the devil must be! How unhappy the Lord must be!

I suggest that you stop looking for a perfect translation—something that you probably won't find. Rather, select the translation that you enjoy most and begin memorizing.

I still find it easiest to memorize from the King James Version. When I find a word that is not clear, I check newer translations and then substitute the word that is more understandable. A number of college students have indicated they prefer memorizing from the King James Version because it is the most familiar.

If you are looking for a newer translation, you have a wide selection. At Georgia State University, researchers compared the readability of the *Good News Bible,* the Revised Standard Version and the King James Version. The *Good News Bible* was rated the most readable. Another comparative test was made at a Christian school in Maryland with students in grades four through eight. The King James Version, the New American Standard and the *New International Version* were compared. The *New International Version* communicated the most clearly.

I am not promoting one particular translation. God can

and does speak through all of them. What I am promoting is your selecting a translation that you find readable and understandable. Then you are ready to begin the venture of memorizing Scripture.

Select the Best Passage

Passages that have meaning to you will be the easiest to memorize. These may be passages that are already familiar or these may be passages that seem unfamiliar but speak to you personally. Selecting a passage that you *want* to memorize gives you a head start in memorizing.

The passage you select may be short or long. It may be one verse, a group of verses, or a chapter. If you decide to memorize individual verses, it is best to select some with a similar theme, or else it may seem as though you are memorizing the dictionary. You constantly change subjects!

Many people begin memorizing by selecting a group of salvation verses. This helps them to better understand their own salvation and aids them in witnessing to others. There are a number of salvation verses in Romans that can become a starting point. These verses, in a progressive order, are 3:23, 6:23, 5:8, 5:1, and 8:1. If you would like added suggestions, most Christian bookstores carry leaflets and booklets which list key verses relating to various subjects.

After memorizing selected verses, you may choose to memorize selected chapters or parts of chapters. A good starting place is in the Psalms. A few favorite psalms would be 1, 23, 24, 46, 84, 100 and 121. Another favorite chapter is 1 Corinthians 13. There are also parts of chapters that form a cluster of verses. These are relatively easy to memorize. Some examples are: Matthew 5:1-12; John 1:1-14; 3:14-18; 14:1-6; Romans 8:1-17; Ephesians 1:15-23; 2:1-10; 6:10-20; Philippians 2:5-11; Colossians 3:1-4; 1 John 1:5-10.

Select the Best Time

If you decide to memorize when you have the time, you are probably deciding not to memorize. Most people do not feel they have free time.

When is the best time? This will differ with different persons, but several considerations are important. First, it should be a time when you can think clearly. To memorize takes concentration and effort. Your mind should be awake and alert.

Second, it should be a time when you are free from distractions. Memorization requires concentration. It is very difficult to concentrate when there are constant sights and sounds to distract your attention.

Third, it should be a time when you feel you have the time. It is difficult to memorize when you feel pressured to be doing something else. Remember, there are 1,440 minutes in every day. Ten minutes a day is not a long time, but in that short amount of time you can make amazing progress.

The key to successful memorization is the ability to remember. Scientists tell us that sleep is necessary to achieve long-term memory. While we sleep, the mind has periods of activity when the things we have just learned are consolidated with what we already know. These scientists have a simple slogan: no sleep, no memory.

An effective pattern is to begin memorizing a verse in the morning. Recall as much of it as possible during the day. Then do additional work in the evening to clarify words or phrases that you cannot recall. During the night, the mind should consolidate what you have learned into your long-term memory. The next morning, you should be able to recall the verse accurately. This sounds simple, doesn't it? Try it. It may be simpler than you imagine.

Read the Passage Aloud and Repeatedly

Our eyes and our ears are the two primary senses we use in learning. Most of what we know has been learned through sight and/or sound. TV commercials are effective because the viewers see a product and hear about its virtues.

When it comes to memorizing the Scriptures, both our eyes and our ears play an important role. We can memorize by reading a verse silently and thinking about it. But we can memorize more rapidly by reading a verse aloud. By both seeing and hearing the verse, our minds are receiving a double impression.

"Read and read; something will be remembered." These are the words of an old Latin proverb and they apply to memorizing. In addition to reading a verse aloud, the verse should be read repeatedly. The repetition gives depth to the double impressions of sight and sound.

Read the Passage Thoughtfully and Prayerfully

When memorizing the Scriptures, the concern is to learn more than words. The concern is to grasp truths that make the Scriptures become alive. How can this be done?

As you read the verse aloud, try to visualize the truths in your mind. Form a mental picture of the key ideas in the verse. This will add an additional impression on your mind. When memorizing Psalm 1, the phrase, "He is like a tree planted by streams of water," was easy to remember. I pictured in my mind the huge trees shading the creek where I went wading in the water as a child.

Furthermore, as you read a verse aloud, pray for an understanding of the truths you are reading. The question Philip asked the Ethiopian eunuch would be appropriate when you are memorizing, "Do you understand what you are reading?" (Acts 8:30b). When you can visualize the ideas of a verse with your mind and understand the truths with your heart, that verse is becoming a part of you. You will soon have it memorized.

When memorizing individual verses, it is helpful to also memorize the reference. There will be times when you will want to turn to these verses in your Bible even though you have them on the tip of your tongue.

Write the Passage

The use of a pencil and paper is valuable at several stages of memorizing. After you are able to repeat a verse without looking at your Bible, writing it helps to clarify the words and phrases. The writing process adds one more level of impression on your mind.

In fact, some people like to begin memorizing by writing a verse on a card and carrying it with them throughout the day. A homemaker can place a Scripture card at the kitchen sink. I have used a Scripture card for memorizing while driving on the highway.

A local Christian barber memorized Scriptures while working in his barbershop. He wrote verses on cards and fastened them on the wall opposite the barber's chair. While at work, he refreshed in his mind the verses he was memorizing. Of course the verses could be read by customers as well.

Review Frequently

No matter how accurately you memorize Scriptures, you will only remember them clearly if you review frequently. An acquaintance memorized the Book of Romans while at work in a factory. He found it necessary to review the entire book once a week to keep it clearly in mind.

Actually, reviewing is the most enjoyable aspect of memorizing Scriptures. To be able to think through verse after

verse or chapter after chapter is both rewarding and enjoyable. In the process, new insights often emerge and one is
refreshed spiritually. One man told me that while shaving
each morning, he reviews verses he has memorized. He is
making double use of his time.

A man who is a long-distance runner, decided to use his
time wisely and review Scriptures he has memorized, while
running. He has now memorized 21 New Testament books.
Jogging time is review time. While he is running mile after
mile, the Scriptures are running through his mind, chapter
after chapter.

A college student who has discovered the rewards of memorizing the Scriptures, agreed to describe his approach to
memorizing and listed the values he has experienced. His
testimony is an inspiring conclusion to this chapter:

> I started memorizing Scripture when a friend asked me to
> try memorizing one verse a day with him. We each chose a
> different passage and agreed to try it for two weeks, meeting
> together daily to recite our verses to each other. That was a
> year and a half ago, and I'm still memorizing a verse a day. I
> have now memorized Romans, James, two chapters in He-
> brews and am working on 2 Timothy.
>
> To memorize a verse, I first read over it several times.
> Then I cover it and try to recite it, checking my accuracy
> line by line as I say it. On longer verses I work through one
> sentence or phrase at a time, repeating the verse from the
> beginning each time I master a new line, until I can say the
> whole verse by memory. I've found that memorizing is
> easier if I can feel and understand what the verse is saying,
> instead of just memorizing a chain of words that don't mean
> anything to me.
>
> Every week or two, I review all the passages I have mem-
> orized, so that I can retain them word for word in my mind.
> It's simple to recite a chapter or two whenever I have some
> spare time, such as walking to school, jogging, or doing work
> that doesn't require much concentration. This is one aspect
> of memorizing that I value highly; that is, being able to med-

itate on Scripture throughout the day during free periods of time, even for just a few minutes. Meditating on Scripture that I have "hidden in my heart" often gives me new insights that I may not have grasped in just reading the passage one time.

Another satisfying aspect of memorization is knowing that what I've memorized cannot be taken away from me, even if the Bible would ever be taken away from me for some reason. Finally, memorization is a very good way to get to know the Bible. Instead of saying, "I'm not sure where it says this, but somewhere in the Bible it says . . .", I can know exactly what the Bible says and where it is found. After all, at this rate, in six more years I could memorize everything from Romans through Jude.

QUESTIONS FOR REFLECTION OR DISCUSSION

1. What verses or passages of Scripture have you memorized? What motivated you to memorize?

2. What new insights about biblical truth have you received while memorizing or while reflecting on Scriptures already memorized?

3. What new uses of Scripture have you found for the passages you have memorized?

4. What are barriers to your memorizing Scripture? Do you see a way of removing these barriers?

8

Systematic Bible Study

"I would like to study the Bible but I cannot go to school. What can I do?" This question is being raised by many people. I have heard it. Perhaps you have too.

My answer to this question has two parts. First, I believe that all persons who want to study the Bible on their own initiative can do it with great value. The classroom is an excellent place for learning but it is not the only place. Second, I would recommend an approach to study called systematic Bible study. This approach is sometimes referred to as inductive Bible study or methodical Bible study. There are many approaches to Bible study and each approach has value. There are many different Bible study materials and most of them can help us to better understand the Bible. But I do not know of any materials or method that equals systematic study.

As the title suggests, systematic Bible study involves following a designated pattern or system when studying an entire book or a particular passage. It involves following a series of steps so that you arrive at an accurate understanding of the Bible and apply its message to your life.

The emphasis is on studying the Bible itself, not books about the Bible. Commentaries have a place but they should not have the central place. Even though Martin Luther wrote many books about the Bible, he felt the Bible should receive our primary attention. Toward the end of his life, he said:

> The Bible is now buried under so many commentaries, that the text is nothing regarded.... Never will the writings of mortal man in any respect equal the sentences inspired by God. We must yield the place of honour to the prophets and the apostles, keeping ourselves prostrate at their feet as we listen to their teachings. I would not have those who read my books, in these stormy times, devote one moment to them which they would otherwise have consecrated to the Bible.[1]

There are various books that explain systematic Bible study. Some of them are so detailed that one can easily become lost in the study process. I have developed a simplified approach that has been helpful to me and to numerous other persons.

In this chapter, I will explain and illustrate systematic study. The study illustrations will be based on 1 John. By reading this chapter you will learn about a helpful method of Bible study and you will also be introduced to the message of 1 John, a most significant New Testament book. As you read this chapter, there will be study assignments. I strongly encourage you to complete them before reading the answers I have given. If you do the assignments, you will better understand this method of Bible study and you will experience the excitement of discovering biblical truth. To read about truths others have discovered is enjoyable, but to discover truth yourself is exciting.

On one occasion, a man said to R. A. Torrey, "Tell me in

a word how to study the Bible." Mr. Torrey replied, "Think." This was good advice. It is the heart of systematic Bible study.

This method has three primary steps: examine, summarize, apply. A major amount of time is devoted to examining the passage being studied. The first question in Bible study is what does the text say? A series of observations help to answer this question. The second question is what message did the author want to give? This question is answered when you summarize the findings of your observations. This is the process of interpretation. The third question is how will I apply the message to my life? The aim of Bible study should always be application. Without application, Bible study loses its God intended purpose.

Let us assume that you now want to learn about 1 John. How should you approach the study of the book? I invite you to follow me step by step. I believe 1 John will become alive and its truths will touch your life. We will first make observations on the entire book to discover its general message. Then we will examine a selected passage to discover and apply its specific message.

Examine the Entire Book
Read the Capsule Information in Chapter 11
Mastering a book of the Bible is like mastering a new subject or area of study. You begin with general information and continue enlarging various areas or details. The capsule of information on 1 John found in chapter 11 of this book provides that general information. Turn now and read the capsule for 1 John. It will only take you about one minute.

Identify the Theme of Each Chapter
You are now ready to begin examining the Book of

1 John. A pencil and paper are necessary tools if you are going to get the greatest benefit from this study. I recommend that you use a notebook for recording your observations and findings.

The first step is to read through the book and record in a word or phrase the theme of each chapter. As you read, do not look for details. Rather, look for the central message. Open your Bible to 1 John and read through the book at one sitting. It will take you about 15 minutes. After reading each chapter, identify in your own words the key theme or message. Record it in your notebook.

Did you find the exercise easy or difficult? If it seemed difficult, don't feel discouraged. It is difficult to identify the one central theme for each chapter in 1 John because there is often more than one theme. I observed that each chapter says something about God and something about God's children. Here are the themes that I observed.

> 1:1-4 Introduction. Jesus Christ, the Word of life.
> 1:5-10 God is light; walk in the light.
> 2:1-29 God is light; abide in the light.
> 3:1-24 God is love; love one another.
> 4:1-21 God is love; abide in love.
> 5:1-21 We know Jesus is God's Son; we know the Son
>   gives life.

Reflecting on the themes of these chapters we observe that 1 John provides teaching on the nature of God as He is revealed in Christ, and teaching on the nature of the Christian life. Furthermore, the nature of the Christian life grows directly out of the nature of God. It is not surprising that John calls Christians "children of God!"

Identify Key Themes of the Book

As you read through 1 John, you probably observed that

certain themes appeared in several chapters. Our knowledge of the book will increase if we identify these themes. I suggest that you lay this book aside and read through 1 John again. As you read, record in your notebook the themes that you observe running through the book.

Again, let's compare our observations. I observed the following four themes:

1. The nature of Jesus Christ.
    He was human (came in the flesh): 1:1-3; 4:1-3.
    He was divine (Son of God): 2:18-27.
2. The character of God and the character of the children of God.
    Light, not darkness: 1:5—2:11.
    Love, not hate: 2:7-11; 3:11-24; 4:7-21.
    Righteousness, not unrighteousness: 2:28—3:10.
3. Christ has conquered sin by providing forgiveness and victory:
    1:5—2:2; 2:12-17; 3:4-10; 4:4-6; 5:4, 5, 18, 19.
4. Christians can *know* if they have eternal life through Christ. How?
    If they obey his commandments: 2:3-5; 5:1-3.
    If they stop practicing sin: 3:4-10.
    If they love other believers: 3:14-15.
    If they possess the Holy Spirit: 3:24; 4:13.

This list does not cover all of the themes and your list may contain some others. But I find these four themes of Jesus, God, sin, and knowledge to be the central ones.

Explore the Historical Setting

Now that you have read through 1 John two times and have begun to get acquainted with the book, you are ready to explore the setting in which the book was written. Why is this valuable? It will help you discover why the book was written and the intended message of the key themes. Some books of the Bible contain specific information about their settings. Others, such as 1 John, reflect the circumstances but they are not specifically stated. If you have a commentary, read the introductory discussion on 1 John. It will help you recreate the setting for the book.

In brief this is what I found from my reading. The Apostle John wrote near the end of the first century. Over 50 years had passed since the Christian church began. During that time, some people who called themselves Christians wanted to mix Christianity and a philosophy called gnosticism.

This philosophy stated that material things were evil but that spiritual things were pure. God, being spirit, was pure and He would have nothing to do with evil material things. Therefore, they concluded that Christ could not have been both God and man. This would have joined spirit which was pure and matter which was evil. Since this belief involved philosophy, they said that salvation came from having a superior knowledge of God, not the death of Christ.

What were the implications of this belief? First, Christ was said to be God but not man. He only appeared to be human. Second, Christ could not have died because He was spirit. Third, faith in the death of Christ could not provide salvation. Fourth, immoral living did not matter. What the material body did would not affect the purity of man's spirit.

Those who held these beliefs were false teachers. Some of them had left the church but others were still teaching this pagan philsophy. John may have been the only apostle living, so he felt a responsibility to write the Christians encouraging them in their faith. In light of this situation, we can understand why John wrote about the nature of Jesus, the character of God, victory over sin, and true knowledge.

But John was interested in more than correcting false teachings. He wrote to increase their fellowship and joy in Christ. The Gospel of John was written to bring people to faith in Christ. This letter was written to help believers know the meaning of that faith.

Examine a Selected Passage

In our study of 1 John, we have now examined the entire book and the historical setting. We have also observed the way in which the setting and the message are related. We are now ready to begin a detailed study of a selected passage. Of course, the entire book could be studied in this way and I would encourage you to do that. However, the purpose of this study is to demonstrate a study method that you can follow in studying any book of the Bible.

Select a Suitable Passage

A passage selected for study should be a basic unit of thought. It might be one paragraph or a group of paragraphs. Many of the newer translations use headings to help identify basic units.

To make this study easy to follow, the passage to be studied is printed below (1 John 3:1-10). We will move through eight simple but important steps in the examining process.

1 How great is the love the Father has lavished on us, that we should be called children of God! And that is what we are! The reason the world does not know us is that it did not know him. 2 Dear friends, now we are children of God, and what we will be has not yet been made known. But we know that when he appears, we shall be like him, for we shall see him as he is. 3 Everyone who has this hope in him purifies himself, just as he is pure.

4 Everyone who sins breaks the law; in fact, sin is lawlessness. 5 But you know that he appeared so that he might take away our sins. And in him is no sin. 6 No one who lives in him keeps on sinning. No one who continues to sin has either seen him or known him.

7 Dear children, do not let anyone lead you astray. He who does what is right is righteous, just as he is righteous. 8 He who does what is sinful is of the devil, because the devil has been sinning from the beginning. The reason the Son of God appeared was to destroy the devil's work. 9 No one who is born of God will continue to sin, because God's seed remains in him; he cannot go on sinning, because he has been born of God. 10 This is how we know who the children of God are and who the children of the devil are: Anyone who does not do what is right is not a child of God; neither is anyone who does not love his brother.

Identify the People

The first step in examining a passage is to identify the people mentioned. This is especially important in studying the gospels but it is helpful in studying other books too. I would again recommend that you follow the assigned steps looking for the information and recording it in your notebook before reading what I have written.

Who are the people mentioned in this passage? Read 1 John 3:1-10 listing those you see. As you list them, define who they are. In this passage, it will be helpful to also identify the terms for God. I observe the following people:

> The Father (1): God the Father.
> Children of God (1, 2, 10): all true Christians including those to whom the letter was written and those who read the letter today.
> Dear friends (2): those to whom he is writing.
> Him (2, 5, 6): Christ, the Son of God.
> Dear children (7): those to whom he is writing.
> The devil (8): Satan.
> Son of God (8): Jesus Christ.
> Children of the devil (10); all unbelievers. Those who are not followers of Jesus Christ.

Notice the affection John had for the people to whom he was writing. Notice also that he wrote to you and me and all believers in Christ.

Check the Meaning of Key Words

The second step is to identify key words in the passage and to check their meanings. These may be unfamiliar words or familiar words that you use but for which you do not know the biblical meaning. After you have listed the key words, check and record their meanings. The best source to check for definitions is a Bible dictionary. If you do not have one available, a standard English dictionary will be a good substitute.

I checked the meaning of the following words:

> lavished (1): to give in great abundance.
> hope (3): to expect something good, especially the return of Christ.
> law (4): God's will for human conduct.
> righteous (7): purity of heart and life.
> seed (9): those who descend from a person or imitate the character of that person.

Now read these verses again, keeping in mind the definitions. Verse three, for example, becomes much clearer. When we live expecting the return of Christ, we are motivated to live a pure life, free from known sin.

Observe the Words that Are Contrasted or Repeated

Key ideas in a passage are highlighted by either repetition or contrast. The third step in examining the passage is to discover the ideas that are emphasized. Read the verses again and record these words or phrases.

I observed the following contrast:

> children of God (1, 2, 10)   children of the devil (10)

The following words are repeated:

> appeared (5, 8)   sin(s) (4, 5, 6, 9)
> appears (2)   sinning (8, 9)

The issue of sin is related to the contrast between the children of God and the children of the devil. It is also related to Christ who appeared as Savior and who will again appear as Judge.

Look for Questions and Answers

The fourth step is to examine the passage to see whether it contains questions and whether those questions are answered. Frequently the author raises questions and provides the answers. Also, an author may be writing in response to questions raised by others. First Corinthians illustrates both approaches. Obviously we understand the answer most accurately if we know the question being asked.

As you read the passage we are studying, you may have noticed that there are no stated questions. There were probably questions in the minds of those to whom the letter was written. The historical setting helps us to know what they might have been. Knowing these questions helps us to understand why John wrote this particular message and helps us to interpret the meaning of this message for us.

To find an example of a question and an answer we only need to read the verses that follow our passage for study. Notice that verse 10 closes with a call to love your brother. The remainder of chapter 3 enlarges this appeal. Verses 11 and 12 read as follows:

> 11 This is the message you heard from the beginning: We should love one another. 12 Do not be like Cain, who belonged to the evil one and murdered his brother. And why did he murder him? Because his own actions were evil and his brother's were righteous.

The question and answer are especially interesting because they relate to a question that has been asked by many people. I have asked it and you may have asked it too. The answer helps us to understand our negative reactions when the life of a righteous person reminds us of the unrighteousness in our lives.

Look for Important Shades of Meaning

In systematic study, each word is significant. To understand the message the author intended, it is helpful to read the passage, slowly reflecting on the individual words looking for the shades of meaning they convey. This fifth step may seem tedious but it can uncover unexpected insights. As you now read the passage, record your findings.

My list included the following:

> Verse 2: now, will be. We are God's children *now*. We do not need to wait until we get to heaven to enjoy this privilege. But Christ is not finished with us yet! Eventually we *will be* like Him! We are to live aware of what we are now but anticipating what we will be. This anticipation influences the way we now live.
>
> Verses 6, 8, 9: continues to sin. In many translations, this phrase is translated "sin" or "commit sin." These words imply that a person needs to be perfect (never sin) to be a Christian. The phrase "continues to sin" is a better translation of the Greek language. It implies that the Christian might slip into sin but that he or she will not practice sin.

Look for Important Connectives

Small, ordinary words can be keys for unlocking the meaning of a verse or passage. The sixth step is to read the passage identifying these small but important words. Here is a list of connectives and the verses in which they are found.

> The AND of progression: (1, 5)
> The BUT of contrast: (2, 5)
> The FOR of reason: (2)
> The AS of comparison: (3)

Other connectives not included in this passage are:

The THEREFORE of conclusion: (see 4:5)
The IF of condition: (see 1:9)

While this list is not exhaustive it does illustrate the way in which small words indicate the thrust of a phrase or sentence. An excellent example is the AS of comparison in verse 3. John says that living with the hope of Christ's return causes us to purify ourselves. But he heightens the call to purity by comparing our level of purity with the purity of Christ. What a calling! What a challenge! How impossible without His life in us!

Check the Mood of the Passage

Every passage of Scripture has a particular mood. A part of the study process is to identify that mood because it helps in discovering the message intended by the author. There are many different moods expressed in the Scriptures. Some of them are listed below.

Praise: many of the Psalms and some of Paul's Epistles have the mood of praise, thanksgiving, or joy.

Despair. The writings of the prophets frequently have the mood of despair. They see the dark clouds of God's judgment on the horizon and know that only God can stop the predicted punishment for their sins.

Hope. The prophets who warned of judgment often concluded their message with confident hope. After judgment and captivity, God would restore His blessings upon His people.

Warning. The Book of Galatians provides a good example of a message with a strong tone of warning. In fact Paul pronounces a curse on those who "preach another Gospel."

Encouragement. Much of the New Testament reflects the mood of nurture or encouragement. The apostles wrote to encourage either a church or a church leader. The emphasis of 1 John is primarily encouragement for the believers with an occasional word of warning against the false prophets. His message had warmth and personal concern for the Christians of his day. We sense the same compassion as we read his message today.

Identify the Literary Style

Passages of Scripture not only have a particular mood, they also have a particular literary style. This too is important in understanding the author's message. The most common examples are as follows:

> *Poetry.* Figurative language found in the Psalms, Job, and sections of the prophets. Truth is presented through word pictures.
>
> *Parable.* A story with one central message. Jesus used parables frequently when He taught His disciples truths that only they could understand. We should seek the one primary message, and not the meaning of the details.
>
> *Apocalyptic.* Writing that uses visions and symbols as in Daniel and Revelation. Many of the symbolisms in Revelation are based on the writings of Old Testament prophets.
>
> *Narrative.* A story or historic account such as much of the Old Testament and Gospels. Narrative is frequently used to report past events of the people of God and the significance of these events.
>
> *Discourse.* A logical presentation of truth. The teachings of Jesus and the Epistles represent this style of writing. First John is a good example of discourse. The author presents his message in a manner designed to inform the mind, warm the heart, and move the will.

Summarize the Teaching of the Passage

A summary statement is intended to bring together the significant observations made while examining the passage. Its purpose is to identify what the author intended to say. It is a part of the interpreting process. Interpretation is determining what the author meant by what he said.

Normally a summary statement of a passage is about one

paragraph in length. It is stating in your own words what you believe the author wanted to say to his audience. I recommend that you now review the findings of the study and record them in brief statements or paragraphs.

In order to illustrate a process, I will first identify key findings from the study and then write a summary paragraph.

Key Findings

The Apostle John is writing to persons whose faith is being challenged by pagan philosophy. He wants them to realize that they are children of God now, and to live a life of obedience to God.

The greatest motivation for pure living is anticipating the return of Christ. He will then make us like Himself. Our calling now is to be pure as He is pure.

It is important that Christians keep a biblical view of who Jesus was. If they give up their belief that He was both God and man, then His death has no meaning for them. They cannot claim forgiveness for past sins or victory over present temptations. They will live like children of the devil who practice sin, thus breaking God's laws. Who we really are is revealed by how we live. We imitate our parents.

Summary Paragraph

This passage calls Christians to remain true to the biblical teachings concerning the nature and ministry of Jesus Christ. Also, it presents a call to obey God's will for human conduct. If we practice the sin of disobedience, this is evidence that we are not children of God.

Apply the Message of the Passage

Application is the final step in the study process. It is putting into life what we have learned with our minds. It is asking the question, what does the passage say to me? (Notice that this question comes at the end of the study, not at the beginning). The Bible was written for all people in every generation. However, not all teachings are intended for all ages.

Types of Teachings

Biblical teachings generally fall into one of three categories.

First, teachings of general truths intended for all believers. These would be teachings that are timeless in value. The Ten Commandments, the teachings of Jesus, and most of the teachings in the Epistles would be examples of teachings for all believers to follow. They would be universal truths.

Second, teachings of local truths intended for specific persons or periods of time. These would be teachings with dated value. Examples of these truths would be Old Testament teachings replaced by the coming of Christ such as the civil and ceremonial laws. A New Testament example would be Paul's instruction to Timothy to drink some wine for his sick stomach (1 Timothy 5:23). Local truths can best be identified by the total message of the Bible.

Third, teachings of general principles that can be applied in all ages. Behind most local truths we find general principles. The general principle behind Paul's instruction to Timothy seems to be the use of medicine for illness.

Application of 1 John Passage

The passage we have been studying in 1 John has teachings of general truth for all believers. They apply to me and to you. The final step for you in this study is to identify how you will apply the message to your own life. Before reading further, record in your notebook what you will do as a result of having studied this passage.

After reflecting on the study of the passage, I have decided on the following applications:

> I intend to live daily aware that I am God's child and that Christ will return to make me like Himself.
> I will hold firm the biblical teaching on who Christ is and what He accomplished in His death and resurrection.
> I will deal honestly with known sin in my life claiming Christ's victory rather than continuing to practice sin.

Your Continuing Study

You have now been exposed to systematic Bible study. At first, the process may seem lengthy and detailed, but it will become simpler with continued use. It yields untold rewards in biblical understanding and personal enrichment. I commend it to your continued use.

If you would like additional information on systematic study, I recommend the book, *The Joy of Discovery in Bible Study*, Revised Edition, by Oletta Wald, published by Augsburg Publishing House.

QUESTIONS FOR REFLECTION OR DISCUSSION

1. What is your reaction to systematic Bible study? Do you feel positive, negative, or neutral? Give reasons for your feelings.

2. In what ways does the present-day situation in our society seem similar to the situation Christians faced when 1 John was written?

3. What truths from 1 John did you apply to your own life as you completed the study? What kind of help will you need to live out the application?

4. What passage of Scripture would you like to study using systematic Bible study? When will you begin that study?

Note

1. Martin Luther, *The Table Talk or Familiar Discourse*, trans. by William Hazlitt (London: David Bogue, 1848), quoted in Edward P. Blair, *The Bible and You* (New York: Abingdon Press, 1953), p. 146.

PART III
AIDS TO SUCCESSFUL
STUDY

9

Favorite Chapters

Every person who reads the Bible can identify certain chapters that have become especially meaningful. These are favorite chapters.

An interesting exercise would be for you to list the five chapters of the Bible that you read most frequently. It might seem difficult since your Bible contains 1,189 chapters. But on further reflection, you will discover that you have an attraction to certain chapters. I would encourage you to stop reading for a few minutes and list your five favorite chapters.

After completing this brief exercise, ask one or more persons to list their favorite chapters also. Compare your lists. Chapters such as Psalm 23 and Romans 8 will probably appear on each list.

Why do certain chapters speak to us more personally than others? If all Scriptures are inspired by the Holy Spirit, why do we have favorite chapters? It is because even though all Scriptures are equally inspired, they are not equally inspiring to us. Some Scriptures speak more directly than others about life as we experience it. Therefore, we feel drawn in a special way to those Scriptures.

In this chapter, I will list a number of favorite chapters of the Bible. Some of the chapters contain verses that are very familiar and verses that are less familiar. The entire chapters will be listed because less familiar verses often add richness to the familiar ones when we discover how they are related.

Take a few minutes to scan over the following listings. Some of them may relate to a present need and you will want to read the suggested chapter or chapters. Others may relate to a need you will encounter in the future. When that time comes, you can return to this listing and find the suggested favorite chapters.

Favorite Chapters Related to Christian Living

Assurance when you are fearful, Psalm 23.
Assurance when you are anxious, Matthew 6.
Comfort when in sorrow, John 14.
Confidence in the midst of danger, Psalm 91.
Confidence when you lack courage, Joshua 1.
Control of the tongue, James 3
Courage when God seems silent, 1 Kings 18.
Encouragement when failed by others, Psalm 27.
Encouragement when tempted to stop witnessing, Jeremiah 20; Ezekiel 33; 2 Corinthians 5; 1 Timothy 4.
Encouragement when tempted to stop worshiping, Daniel 6; Amos 7.
Encouragement when discipleship seems too costly, 2 Corinthians 11; 2 Timothy 4; Hebrews 12.
Faith when faced with tragedy, Job 1, 38, 42.
Forgiveness when others fail you, Philemon
Formula when you desire to bear fruit, John 15.
Gratitude when you forget your blessings, Psalm 103; Philippians 4.
Humility of mind and spirit, Philippians 2.
Instructions when you forget kingdom standards, Matthew 5—7.
Love when you become critical and cold, 1 Corinthians 13; 1 John 3.
Motivation when your faith is failing, Hebrews 11.

Preparation when you worship, Psalm 84, 100; Revelation 5.
Preparation when you observe the Lord's Supper,
    1 Corinthians 11.
Protection when surrounded by enemies, Ezra 8; Isaiah 36,
    37.
Realism when you desire pleasure more than God,
    Ecclesiastes 2.
Reconciliation when divided by prejudice, Ephesians 2.
Repentance when you have sinned, Psalm 51.
Security when you feel insecure, Isaiah 40.
Sensitivity toward weaker Christians, Romans 14.
Stimulation when your giving to God ceases, Malachi 3;
    2 Corinthians 9.
Unselfish deeds for other's needs, Esther 5.
Victory when you are defeated by sin, Romans 6, 8;
    Ephesians 6.
Warning when sin becomes attractive, Judges 2; 2 Samuel
    12; Romans 1.

Favorite Chapters About God

His creative acts, Genesis 1, 2.
His majesty, Psalm 8.
His eternal nature, Psalm 90.
His sovereign power, Jeremiah 18; Zechariah 14.
His love and patience, Lamentations 3; Hosea 11; Jonah 4;
    John 3.
His desire for righteousness and justice above religious
    rituals, Amos 5; Micah 6.
His justice toward all men, Ezekiel 18; Habakkuk 2.
His unlimited resources, Haggai 2.
His great invitation, Isaiah 55.
His protection of his faithful people, 2 Kings 19; Psalm 121
His presence in times of trouble, Psalm 46.
His gift of wisdom, 2 Chronicles 9.
His victory over Satan, Revelation 20.
His new heaven and new earth, Revelation 21, 22.

Favorite Chapters About Christ

His birth prophesied, Isaiah 7, 9.
His death prophesied, Isaiah 53.
His birth described, Matthew 1, 2; Luke 2.

His temptation, Matthew 4; Luke 4.
His concern for our total needs, Mark 6.
His ministry, Matthew 5—7.
His parables, Matthew 13; Mark 4; Luke 15—18.
His power over death, John 11.
His death described, Matthew 27; Mark 15; Luke 23;
     John 19.
His resurrection, Matthew 28; Mark 16; Luke 24; John 20.
His promise of our resurrection, 1 Corinthians 15.
His importance for our salvation, Galatians 3; Colossians 1.
His second coming, Matthew 25; 1 Thessalonias 4;
     2 Thessalonians 2; 2 Peter 3.

Favorite Chapters About the Holy Spirit

His presence promised by Jesus, John 14, 16.
His coming at Pentecost, Acts 2.
His gifts to the church, 1 Corinthians 12; Ephesians 4.
The fruit he produces, Galatians 5.

Favorite Chapters About Prayer

David's prayer of gratitude, 1 Chronicles 29.
Solomon's dedication prayer, 2 Chronicles 6.
The Lord's Prayer, Matthew 6.
Christ's prayer for his followers, John 17.
Peter delivered by prayer, Acts 12.
Paul's prayer for our knowledge, Ephesians 1.
Prayer and healing, James 5.

Favorite Chapters About Marriage and Family

Designed by God, Genesis 2.
Instruction for wives, Proverbs 31.
Adoration of the bridegroom for the bride,
     Song of Solomon 4.
Forgiveness for unfaithfulness, Hosea 3.
God's displeasure with divorce, Malachi 2; Mark 10.
Parents' responsibility to teach their children,
     Deuteronomy 6.
The church's responsibility toward widows, Ruth 2.
God's pattern for family life, Ephesians 5, 6.

QUESTIONS FOR REFLECTION OR DISCUSSION

1. Which are your five favorite chapters? What special message does each chapter speak to you?

2. Can you recall when each of these chapters became a favorite? What was the circumstance?

3. Is your list of favorite chapters changing? Which chapters, if any, are no longer your favorites?

4. As you read over the listing of chapters, which ones relate to present needs?

10

Bible Chronology

The books of the Old Testament are arranged in an exact historical order. True or false?

I recall the first time I read through the Old Testament. I assumed that the books were in chronological order and that I would not read the end of Old Testament history until reading Malachi, the last Old Testament book. I was surprised to find Ezra and Nehemiah describing the end of the Old Testament period, since they are located approximately in the middle of the Old Testament.

This chapter contains several charts that will help you understand the history of the Bible and where the many books of the Bible fit into that history. A brief explanation of the charts will make them more useful.

Turn to "The Old Testament at a Glance." The top line identifies the various periods and corresponding dates. A few minutes of reflection should be sufficient to learn these periods. This will help you understand the Old Testament.

The second line identifies key persons and events. You will see a number of familiar names such as Abraham and David, and you can tell when they lived. Of special interest is the divided kingdom after the death of Solomon. The Northern kingdom was called Israel and the Southern kingdom Judah. The capital of Judah was Jerusalem and the capital of Israel was Samaria. The chart shows when each capital was captured and Judah's return from captivity. Another chart lists the kings of Judah and Israel.

The third section of the chart identifies the three groupings of Old Testament books and where they fit into Old Testament history. The line under each book indicates the period of time covered by that book. You will observe that the period of time covered by Genesis is quite long and the number of years covered by Deuteronomy is quite short. Generally the books of history cover many years but the books of poetry and prophecy cover relatively few years.

The second chart, "Kings and Prophets of Judah and Israel," lists the kings and dates of their reigns. In some cases, you will notice the dates for two kings overlapping. This indicates either co-regency or claim to the throne. The lines under certain kings of Israel indicates the nine dynasties. Israel's kings were disobedient to God and experienced much violence. Eight of the kings were slain or committed suicide. Israel lasted only 209 years. In contrast, Judah had some kings that were obedient to God. It has only one dynasty and lasted 345 years.

The center column of the chart identifies the prophets at the times of their prophetic ministries. More information about the prophets can be found in the capsules of information in chapter 11.

The third chart, "The New Testament at a Glance," provides an outline for the New Testament similar to the chart for the Old Testament. Since the period of time is much shorter there are fewer periods. Remember that the lines under the events and books indicate the period of time

THE OLD TESTAMENT AT A GLANCE

Periods	Patriarchs				Bondage in Egypt					Judges
2000BC	1900	1800	1700	1600	1500	1400	1300	1200	1100	

Persons & Events

EXODUS *

Abraham *   Isaac *   Jacob / *   Joseph *

Moses / * *   Joshua /   Samuel \ * *   Samson

O.T. Books

Genesis

Exodus

Leviticus

Numbers

1 Samuel

History

Deuteronomy

Joshua

Judges

Ruth

Poetry

Job?

Prophecy

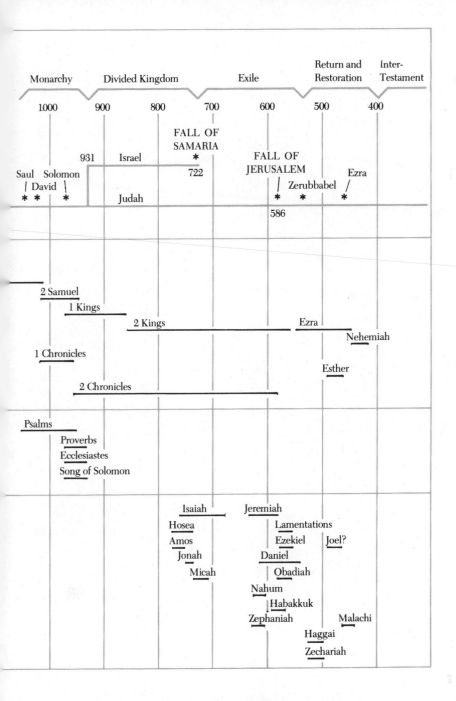

Monarchy   Divided Kingdom   Exile   Return and Restoration   Inter-Testament

1000   900   800   700   600   500   400

FALL OF SAMARIA
*
722

931   Israel

FALL OF JERUSALEM

Ezra

Saul   Solomon
| David \
* * | *

Zerubbabel
*   *   *

Judah

586

2 Samuel
1 Kings
2 Kings
Ezra
Nehemiah
1 Chronicles
Esther
2 Chronicles

Psalms
Proverbs
Ecclesiastes
Song of Solomon

Isaiah   Jeremiah
Hosea   Lamentations
Amos   Ezekiel   Joel?
Jonah   Daniel
Micah   Obadiah
Nahum
Habakkuk
Zephaniah   Malachi
Haggai
Zechariah

PROPHETS AND KINGS OF JUDAH AND ISRAEL

KINGS OF JUDAH	Reign	PROPHETS
Saul	1045-1010 BC	Samuel
David	1010-970	
Solomon	970-931	
Kingdom Divided		
Rehoboam	931-913	
Abijam	913-910	
Asa	910-870	
Jehoshaphat	873-848	Elijah
Jehoram	853-841	
Ahaziah	841	
Athaliah	841-835	Elisha
Joash	835-796	
Amaziah	796-767	
Uzziah	790-740	Amos
Jotham	751-732	
		Hosea
		Isaiah
		Micah
Ahaz	735-716	Jonah
Hezekiah	728-687	
Manasseh	692-642	
Amon	642-640	
Josiah	639-609	Zephaniah
		Nahum
Jehoiahaz	609	Jeremiah
Jehoiakim	608-597	Habakkuk
Jehoiachin	597	Obadiah
Zedekiah	597-587	Daniel (in Babylon)
FALL OF JERUSALEM	586	Ezekiel (in Babylon)
Return with Zerubbabel	538	
	520	Haggai
		Zechariah
Return with Ezra	458	Joel
	450	Malachi
Return of Nehemiah	445	

Reign	KINGS OF ISRAEL
931-910	Jeroboam I
910-909	Nadab
909-886	Baasha
886-885	Elah
885	Zimri
885-874	Omri
874-853	Ahab
853-852	Ahaziah
852-841	Jehoram
841-814	Jehu
814-796	Jehoahaz
798-782	Joash
793-753	Jeroboam II
753	Zechariah
752	Shallum
752-742	Memahem
741-740	Pekahiah
752-732	Pekah
731-722	Hoshea
722	FALL OF SAMARIA

THE NEW TESTAMENT AT A GLANCE

Periods	The Life of Jesus				

	4 BC	AD 27	28	29	30

Events

Judean Ministry

Galilean Ministry

Perean Ministry

To Jerusalem Ministry

Birth, Childhood
*

Baptism
*

Death & Resurrection
*

N.T. Books

Gospels

Matthew

Mark

Luke

John

History

Epistles

Prophecy

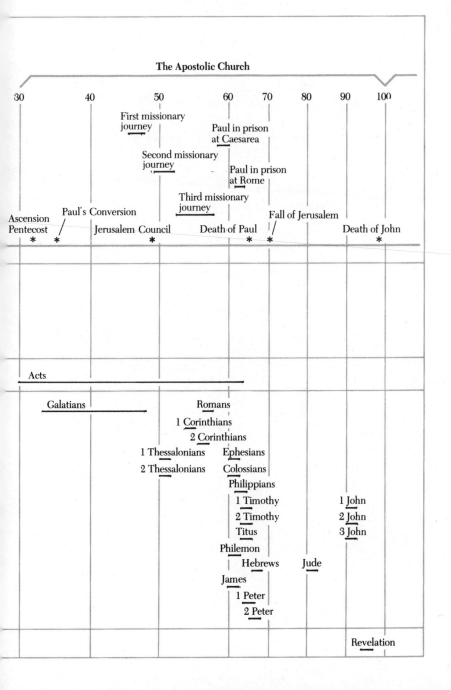

The Apostolic Church

30	40	50	60	70	80	90	100

First missionary journey

Paul in prison at Caesarea

Second missionary journey

Paul in prison at Rome

Third missionary journey

Paul's Conversion

Fall of Jerusalem

Ascension
Pentecost   Jerusalem Council   Death of Paul   Death of John

Acts

Galatians

Romans

1 Corinthians

2 Corinthians

1 Thessalonians   Ephesians

2 Thessalonians   Colossians

Philippians

1 Timothy   1 John

2 Timothy   2 John

Titus   3 John

Philemon

Hebrews   Jude

James

1 Peter

2 Peter

Revelation

covered. Notice the Epistles and the way they are grouped in a short period of time.

Spend some time examining these charts. Look for new insights that you can discover about the Bible. You will want to return to these charts many times to help "fit the pieces together."

QUESTIONS FOR REFLECTION OR DISCUSSION

1. As you examined the Old Testament chart, what new insights did you receive? What new questions did it raise that you want to explore?

2. The list of kings and prophets indicates that there was a relationship between the disobedience of the kings and the presence of the prophets. How are these two related?

3. What new understandings did you receive from the New Testament chart? Why did Paul make such a great contribution as a missionary and author of Epistles?

11

Capsule of Each Book of the Bible

Each book of the Bible was written for a specific purpose and is therefore different from all other books. Before reading or studying a book of the Bible, it is helpful to have some information about its setting and its message.

This chapter provides this type of summary information. If you spend one minute reading the capsule information before you read a book, your venture into that book will be more interesting and rewarding.

The 39 Old Testament books are divided into three main groups: History, Poetry, and Prophecy. The first 17 books, Genesis through Esther, are historical. They trace the Old Testament period from the beginning of the world, to the beginning of the Hebrew race, to their possession of the Promised Land, to their captivity in Babylon and their eventual return to the land. While the first five books are sometimes called the books of the law, they also include important information about the early history of the people of the world and the people of God. It is therefore suitable to include them with the books of history.

The five books, Job through Song of Solomon, are the

books of poetry. In addition to being in poetic form, Proverbs and Ecclesiastes are also Wisdom literature. They set forth in brief, concise, statements the wisdom of Israel and the author.

Hebrew poetry is different than traditional English poetry. It does not have the sense of rhyme that we associate with poetry. Rather, Hebrew poetry has parallelism which is the pattern of having two related statements. The first line states a truth and the second line either restates the same thought in different words or states a contrasting truth. There is a rhythm of ideas rather than sounds.

The last 17 books of the Old Testament, Isaiah through Malachi, are the books of prophecy. The first five books are called the major prophets and the last 12 the minor prophets. These 12 books are shorter in length than the major prophets and the prophets are not as well known.

Throughout its history, Israel strayed from the pathway of obedience to its covenant with God. The task of the prophets was to call the people to repentance and obedience to God's will. The prophet's task was usually difficult because his message of judgment was unpopular and therefore unwanted. Yet with God's sustaining strength, the prophets were faithful in proclaiming their, "Thus saith the Lord." Their task was to forthtell and to foretell. The primary task was to tell forth God's call to repentance. The secondary task was to foretell future events.

The 27 New Testament books are divided into four categories: Biography, History, Epistles or Letters, and Prophecy. The first four books, Matthew through John, are biographical books, also called the Gospels. They present the life of Christ, each from a particular point of view. The first three are called synoptic Gospels because they are similar. The Gospel of John is strikingly different from the synoptics.

The capsules will identify some of the differences.

The New Testament has only one book of history, The Acts of the Apostles. It describes the beginning of the Christian church at Jerusalem and traces the spread of the gospel of Jesus Christ from Jerusalem to Rome.

There are 21 Epistles or Letters, Romans through Jude. These are divided into three groups: Romans through 2 Thessalonians, letters of Paul to churches; 1 Timothy through Philemon, letters of Paul to persons; Hebrews through Jude, General Epistles or Letters.

The Epistles were written in response to needs and problems of the early church. They therefore provide a window to the early years of the Christian movement. In addition, they contain the basic teachings of the apostles. These teachings tell us what the apostles believed and how they expected Christians to live.

Revelation, the last book in the New Testament, is a book of prophecy. It is the Revelation of Jesus Christ. This includes a revelation about Christ's place in the church today and a revelation of Christ's plan for our world. While this book has the widest variety of interpretations, it also has some of the most significant truths for our day.

The remainder of this chapter presents, in capsule form, basic information about each book of the Bible including author, date, theme, content, and key chapters. This information can be used in several ways. First, you may wish to read this condensed information to give you a "feel" of each book. Second, you may wish to read the capsule of information about a particular book before reading that book in the Bible. It will then be easier to understand what you read. Third, you may choose to read the key chapters in each book of the Bible. This will give you a "taste" of each book even if you do not read the book in its entirety.

Bible scholars find it difficult to be certain of the exact dates of some earlier Old Testament events. It is also difficult to be certain of the dates when some Old Testament and some New Testament books were written. I have chosen to follow fairly closely the dates indicated in the *Eerdmans' Handbook to the Bible*. This book contains a more complete discussion of each book of the Bible.

GENESIS

Author
The principal author was Moses. For a discussion on the authorship of the first five books of the Old Testament, see the article on "Moses and the Pentateuch" in *The New Bible Commentary: Revised*.

Date
Period covered: from creation to about 1700 BC. Date written: about 1280 to 1240 BC.

Theme
Genesis is the book of beginnings. Chapters 1 to 11 describe the beginning of the world, the human race, sin, family life, civilization, and nations. Chapters 12 to 50 tell about the beginning of the Hebrew race.

Contents
The book contains ten stories: 1—4, The creation of the universe and the fall of man; 5—6:8, Adam; 6:9—9, Noah; 10—11:9, The sons of Noah; 11:10—26, Shem; 11:27—25:11, Abraham; 25:12—18, Ishmael; 25:19—35, Isaac; 36, Esau; 37—50, Jacob.

Key Chapters
1, 2, Creation; 3, The Fall; 12, Call of Abraham; 15, 17, Abrahamic covenant; 45, Joseph and his brothers.

EXODUS

Author
The author was Moses.

Date
    Period covered: about 1365 to 1280 BC. Date written: about 1280 to 1240 BC.

Theme
    Exodus is the book of redemption. God redeemed or delivered Israel from their oppression in Egypt. This deliverance is called the Exodus. It was an act of redemption and symbolizes all of God's redemptive deeds for His people. Exodus begins with the birth of Moses and concludes with Israel building the tabernacle in the wilderness.

Contents
    1—11, Oppression in Egypt; 12—14, Deliverance from Egypt; 15—18, Testing in the wilderness; 19—34, The law and the covenant; 35—40, Building the tabernacle.

Key Chapters
    2, Birth of Moses; 3, Call of Moses; 12, Passover; 20, Ten Commandments.

LEVITICUS

Author
    The author was Moses.

Date
    Period covered and date written: about 1280 to 1240 BC.

Theme
    Leviticus is the book of worship. Moses instructs priests about conducting worship at the tabernacle. A key emphasis is, "Be holy, for I am holy."

Contents
    1—7, Sacrificial offerings; 8—10, The priesthood; 11—16, Purification from uncleanness; 17—22, A call to holiness; 23—27, Patterns of worship.

Key Chapters
    16, Day of atonement; 23, Five festivals; 25, Year of jubilee.

NUMBERS

Author
    The author was Moses.

Date
Period covered and date written: about 1280 to 1240 BC.

Theme
While Numbers is called the book of wanderings, its name comes from two census experiences for Israel (1:2 and 26:2). Before leaving Sinai, Israel conducted a military census because they were to soon enter the land promised to Abraham, Isaac, and Jacob. The second census was conducted after the forty years in the wilderness.

Contents
1—10:10, Preparation for wilderness travel; 10:11—21, Wilderness wanderings; 22—25, Balaam and Israel; 26—36, Preparation for entering Canaan.

Key Chapters
13, Spies return; 14, Moses intercedes for Israel; 20, Moses strikes the rock; 21, The fiery serpent.

DEUTERONOMY

Author
The author was Moses.

Date
Period covered and date written: about 1260 to 1240 BC.

Theme
Deuteronomy is the book of obedience. The name means "second law." While the book is a restating of parts of the law, it adds a spiritual understanding to both the laws and historic events. It calls for a strong spiritual life stressing faith and obedience. It contains the final words of Israel's greatest leader.

Contents
1—4, Moses' first address on Israel's past; 5—26, Moses' second address on blessings and cursings; 27—30, Moses' third address on Covenant renewal; 31—34, Moses' final days and death.

Key Chapters
6, Command to teach; 18, The messianic prophet; 26, Israel's creed; 29, 30, Covenant blessings; 34, Death of Moses.

JOSHUA

Author
The author was likely Joshua and "elders who outlived Joshua" (Joshua 24:31).

Date
Period covered: about 1240 to 1220 BC. Date written: about 1230 to 1220 BC or later.

Theme
Joshua is the book of conquest. Moses died within sight of the Promised Land. Joshua became his successor and led Israel across the Jordan and into Canaan.

Contents
1—5, Entering Canaan; 6—12, Conquest of Canaan; 13—22, Dividing the land; 23—24, Joshua's last days.

Key Chapters
1, God's commission to Joshua; 3, Crossing the Jordan; 7, The sin of Achan; 24, Joshua's farewell.

JUDGES

Author
The author is unknown, perhaps Samuel or his prophets.

Date
Period covered: about 1220 to 1050 BC. Date written: about 1050 BC.

Theme
Judges is the book of failure. Numerous times Israel repeated the cycle of worshiping other gods, captivity, repentance and deliverance. Deliverance came through the leadership of a judge and the power of God. Thirteen judges are identified.

Contents
1—3:6, The period of the judges introduced; 3:7-11, Othniel; 3:12-30, Ehud; 3:31, Shamgar; 4—5, Deborah and Barak; 6—9, Gideon; 10:1, 2, Tola; 10:3-5, Jair; 10:6—12:7, Jephthah; 12:8-10, Ibzan; 12:11, 12, Elon; 12:13-15, Abdon; 13—16, Samson.

Key Chapters
2, The pattern of the judges; 6, Gideon and the fleece; 16 Samson and Delilah.

RUTH

Author
The author is unknown.

Date
Period covered: about 1170 to 1150 BC. Date written: about 1150 BC or later.

Theme
Ruth is the book of kinsman-redeemer. Through the obligation of a kinsman, Boaz the Hebronite and Ruth the widowed Moabitess marry. Their son, Obed, was the grandfather of David. Jesus, the Redeemer, was the "son of David."

Contents
1, Naomi and Ruth go to Bethlehem; 2, Ruth gleans in the field of Boaz; 3, Boaz discovers kinship; 4, The marriage of Ruth and Boaz.

Key Chapters
1, Ruth's dedication to her mother-in-law, Naomi; 4, Boaz "redeems" Ruth through marriage.

1 SAMUEL

Author
The author was Samuel and other authors (1 Chronicles 29:29).

Date
Period covered: about 1090 to 1010 BC. Date written: about 1025 BC and later.

Theme
First Samuel is the book of Ṣamuel and Saul. It records the transition from a theocracy (a nation with God as King) to a monarchy (a nation with a human king). Samuel was the last of the judges and the first of the prophets.

Contents
1—7:14, Samuel's early years; 7:15—15, Saul, Israel's first king; 16—31, The rise of David.

Key Chapters
2, Samuel's dedication to God; 3, Samuel's call from God; 10, Samuel anoints Saul to be king; 18, Jonathan and David make a covenant.

2 SAMUEL

Author
See 1 Samuel.

Date
Period covered: about 1010 to 970 BC. Date written: about 990 BC and later.

Theme
Second Samuel is the book of David. It traces his life from the death of Saul to the latter years of his reign. In spite of his failures, David was a "man after God's own heart."

Contents
1—9, David's early reign; 10—15:6, David's military successes and moral failure; 15:7—18:18, Absalom's rebellion and defeat; 18:19—24, David's return to power and final reign.

Key Chapters
5, David is anointed king; 7, God's promise to David; 11, David's great sin; 12, David repents.

1 KINGS

Author
The author is unknown. Some of the sources for writing are identified in 1 Kings 11:41; 14:19, 29.

Date
Period covered: about 970 to 850 BC. The kingdom was divided about 930 BC. Date written: about 590 to 550 BC.

Theme
First Kings is the book of Solomon and the first number of kings of Israel and Judah. The kings of Israel are compared with King Jeroboam of Israel who turned away from the covenant. The kings of Judah are compared with King David who followed the covenant.

Contents
1—11, The reign of Solomon; 12—14, The kingdom divides;

15—22, War and friendship between Israel and Judah and the ministry of Elijah.

Key Chapters
3, Solomon's prayer for wisdom; 8, Solomon's prayer at the temple dedication; 18, Elijah's contest with the prophets of Baal on Mount Carmel.

2 KINGS

Author
See 1 Kings

Date
Period covered: about 850 to 560 BC. Samaria, the capital of Israel, fell to Assyria in 722 BC. Jerusalem, the capital of Judah, fell to Babylon in 586 BC. Date written: about 590 to 550 BC.

Theme
Second Kings is the book of the latter kings of Judah and Israel. (See 1 Kings for additional information.)

Contents
1—17, The ministry of Elisha and the end of the Kingdom of Israel; 18—21, Judah faces the Assyrian Empire; 22—23:30, The reforms of Josiah; 23:31—25, Judah's final days.

Key Chapters
2, Elisha replaces Elijah; 4, Elisha begins his miracle ministry; 19, Hezekiah's God defeats the Assyrians; 20, God's promise to Hezekiah.

1 CHRONICLES

Author
The principal author was Ezra. First and second Chronicles, Ezra, and Nehemiah likely had the same author as they were originally one book.

Date
Period covered: about 1010 to 970 BC. Date written: about 460 to 440 BC.

Theme
First Chronicles is the book of the first king of Judah, David. He is shown as the father of a spiritual rather than a secular kingdom.

Contents
1—9, The history of man before David's time; 10—29, The reign of David.

Key Chapters
22, David prepares to build the temple; 29, A prayer of David.

2 CHRONICLES

Author
The principal author was Ezra.

Date
Period covered: about 970 to 586 BC. Date written: about 460 to 440 BC.

Theme
Second Chronicles is the book of the kings of Judah. It begins with Solomon who was the second king and concludes with Josiah who was the last king. The temple, priesthood, and moral law are emphasized. The story of the ten apostate tribes of Israel is omitted.

Contents
1—9, Solomon's reign; 10—36, The kingdom of Judah.

Key Chapters
6, Solomon's prayers; 9, Solomon's wisdom; 20, God delivers Judah from her enemies.

EZRA

Author
The principal author was Ezra.

Date
Period covered: about 538 to 457 BC. Date written: about 460 to 440 BC.

Theme
Ezra is the book of return from captivity. God caused King Cyrus to allow the Jews to return to Jerusalem to rebuild the city and the temple. Ezra became a leader in Jerusalem.

Contents
1—2, Return from exile; 3—4:5, Rebuilding begun; 4:6-24,

Rebuilding stopped through opposition; 5—6, Temple completed; 7—8, Ezra's mission and journey; 9—10, The problem of mixed marriages.

Key Chapters
3, The excitement of rebuilding the temple; 8, God protects those returning from exile.

NEHEMIAH

Author
The principal author was Ezra.

Date
Period covered: about 445 to 410 BC. Date written: about 440 to 410 BC.

Theme
Nehemiah is the book of reforms. He rallied the people to rebuild the walls of Jerusalem, in spite of intense opposition. The city was then inhabited and the law read to bring about spiritual reform.

Contents
1—2:11, Nehemiah returns to Jerusalem; 2:12—7:4, The wall is rebuilt; 7:5—12:26, The Covenant of obedience; 12:27—13, Worship and reforms.

Key Chapters
4, Building in adversity; 8, Ezra reads the book of the law; 9, A prayer of repentance.

ESTHER

Author
The author is unknown.

Date
Period covered and date written: about 485 to 465 BC.

Theme
Esther is the book of divine providences. God is Sovereign over circumstances that threatened the very existence of His chosen people. Just as an evil person, Haman, plotted the death of the Jews, so a righteous person, Esther, risked the possibility of death and secured life for the Jewish race.

Contents
1, Queen Vashti demoted; 2, Esther promoted as the new queen; 3, Haman's plot; 4—5:8, Esther intercedes; 5:9—7, Haman is hanged; 8—10, Mordecai is promoted by the king.

Key Chapters
5, Queen Esther's unselfish deed; 7, Haman reaps what he has sown.

JOB

Author
The author is unknown.

Date
Period covered and date written: estimates vary from 1800 to 600 BC.

Theme
Job is the book of faith in affliction. It provides a theological interpretation of the suffering of Job. It reveals for all time that suffering is not always the result of personal sin. Furthermore, a personal revelation of God removes our demand for an explanation of our suffering. The book is a universal poem. It speaks to all generations.

Contents
1—2, Job's loss; 3—37, The explanations of Job's friends; 38—41, The Lord speaks to Job; 42, Job's response and restoration.

Key Chapters
1—2, Job's prosperity and Satan's challenge; 23, Job's appeal to God; 38, God responds to Job; 42, Job responds to God.

PSALMS

Author
The principal author was David. The sons of Korah and Asaph also wrote psalms.

Date
Period covered and date written: about 1000 BC with some as late as 600 BC.

Theme
Psalms is the book of praises. The central theme is God, not

man. About one half of the psalms are prayers of faith during times of trouble. About forty are psalms of praise. God is seen as the Creator of the universe, the Lord of Israel and the sovereign King in this world.

Contents
The 150 psalms are divided into five books, each concluding with a doxology. The groupings are general with not all psalms in each book on the same theme. 1—41 and 42—72, Prayers of faith in times of trouble; 73—89, Psalms of trust in national distress; 90—106, Psalms of praise; 107—150, Psalms of praise and trust.

Key Chapters
1, 116 Psalms of righteousness; 2, 45, 110, Royal psalms; 8, 19, 24, 100, 103, Psalms of praise; 23, 91, 121, Psalms of trust; 32, 51, Psalms of repentance.

PROVERBS

Author
The principal author was Solomon.

Date
Period covered and date written: about 970 to 930 BC with some earlier and some later.

Theme
Proverbs is the book of wisdom. Wisdom comes from God and is given to those who follow God's ways. The "fear of the Lord" is the essence of wisdom.

Contents
1—9, Lessons on wisdom; 10—22:16, and 25—29, The wisdom of Solomon; 22:17—24 and 30—31:9, Words of wisdom; 31:10-31, The perfect wife.

Key Chapters
3, The happiness of wisdom; 24, Solomon's choice words; 31, Praise of a good wife.

ECCLESIASTES

Author
The author was probably Solomon.

Date
Period covered and date written: about 970 to 930 BC or later.

Theme
Ecclesiastes is the book of human experience. When life is lived apart from God and to satisfy all personal desires, then life is described in the phrase, "Vanity of vanities, all is vanity."

Contents
1—4, Life without meaning; 5—6, Religion and life; 7—8, In search of wisdom; 9, The fate of death; 10—11, Proverbs about life; 12, Advice to youth.

Key Chapters
2, A search for pleasure; 3, A time for everything; 12, Remember God in your youth.

THE SONG OF SOLOMON

Author
The author was Solomon.

Date
Period covered and date written: between 970 and 930 BC.

Theme
The Song of Solomon is the book of human love. It describes the pure love that developed between Solomon and a country maiden (Shulamite) which developed into devotion and marriage.

Contents
1—2:7, Solomon meets the maiden; 2:8—3:5, Their love deepened; 3:6—5:1, The marriage; 5:2—8, Brief absence and happy reunion.

Key Chapters
2, The budding of love; 4, The bridegroom adores the bride.

ISAIAH

Author
The author was Isaiah

Date
Period covered and date written: about 740 to 680 BC or later.

Theme

Isaiah is the book of the Messiah. He is known as the evangelical prophet because he gives the clearest picture of the Christ to be found in the Old Testament. God is sovereign as Creator of the universe and Lord of history. In his own time, His servant will come, born of a virgin. He will be a light to all people, including the Gentiles.

Content

1—5, Rebuke and promise for Judah and Jerusalem; 6, Isaiah's call; 7—12, Immanuel and Assyria; 13—23, Judgment on the nations; 24—27, God's final victory; 28—33, Judgment on Israel; 34—35, Judgment and promise; 36—39, Hezekiah is tested; 40—48, The Messiah as Comforter; 49—57, The Messiah as Servant; 58—66, The Messiah as Redeemer.

Key Chapters

6, The prophet's call; 7, 9, A son is born; 53, The suffering servant; 55, The great invitation.

JEREMIAH

Author

The author was Jeremiah.

Date

Period covered: about 627 to 586 BC. Date written: about 600 to 586 BC.

Theme

Jeremiah is the book of pleading and pity. For 40 years, Jeremiah warned Judah of coming judgment and called for repentance. Refusing to repent, God brought judgment through Nebuchadnezzar, King of Babylon. In 587, Jerusalem was destroyed and the people were taken captive into exile in Babylon. Jeremiah remained in Judah but was later taken to Egypt where, it is believed, he spent the rest of his life.

Contents

1—25, God's message to Judah and Jerusalem; 26—45, Jeremiah's life and ministry; 46—52, Prophecies against foreign nations.

Key Chapters

1, The prophet's call; 31, The new covenant; 39, 52, The fall of Jerusalem.

LAMENTATIONS

Author
The author appears to be Jeremiah.

Date
Period covered: about 586 to 580 BC. Date written: about 586 BC or later.

Theme
Lamentations is the book of mourning. Jerusalem was a city of beauty and religious significance, it was the city of God. It's destruction brought deep grief because of the suffering of the people and the loss of the temple which symbolized God's rejection of His people.

Contents
Each chapter is a lament. 1, Jerusalem is destroyed; 2, Israel's enemies rejoice; 3, God is still love; 4, The price of human sin; 5, A prayer for restoration.

Key Chapters
3, God's love in the midst of judgment; 5, Hope in the midst of punishment.

EZEKIEL

Author
The author was Ezekiel.

Date
Period covered and date written: about 590 to 570 BC.

Theme
Ezekiel is the book of overthrow and restoration. At about 25 years of age Ezekiel was taken captive to Babylon. Five years later, God called him to serve as a prophet. He began with a message of judgment. After the temple was destroyed, his message changed to God's restoration of Israel.

Contents
1—24, Judgment on Israel and Jerusalem; 25—32, Judgment on foreign nations; 33—48, Israel's restoration.

Key Chapters
1—3, Ezekiel's call; 10, Vision of the wheels; 37, The valley of dry bones.

DANIEL

Author
The author was Daniel.

Date
Period covered and date written: about 605 to 538 BC.

Theme
Daniel is the book of dreams and visions. The prophetic ministry of Daniel took place in Babylon where he had been taken into exile as a youth. Through the blessing of God, Daniel became both a prophet and a statesman. He was God's representative in the court of pagan kings.

Contents
1—6, Experiences in the Babylonian court; 7—12, Visions of future events.

Key Chapters
3, The fiery furnace; 6, Daniel in the lions' den; 9, Daniel's prayer for his people.

HOSEA

Author
The author was Hosea.

Date
Period covered and date written: 760 to 722 BC.

Theme
Hosea is the book of unfaithfulness and backsliding. The prophet's message was for Israel, the Northern kingdom, during its final years before it fell to Assyria. Hosea's wife became unfaithful and yet Hosea took her back and forgave her sin. Out of this family tragedy, the prophet called Israel back from her unfaithfulness to God.

Contents
1—3, Hosea's tragic home life; 4—10, the coming judgment; 11—14, God's suffering love.

Key Chapters
3, Hosea buys back his unfaithful wife; 11, The mercy of God.

JOEL

Author
    The author was Joel.

Date
    Period covered and date written: exact date is unknown with opinions ranging from the eighth to the fourth century BC.

Theme
    Joel is the book of Pentecost. Following a locust invasion that devastated Judah, Joel spoke God's message of the coming day of the Lord, the day of God's judgment. Beyond judgment there would be a day of God's blessing when He would pour out His Spirit on all flesh.

Contents
    1—2:27, The locust plague and restoration; 2:28—3, The day of the Lord and God's future blessing.

Key Chapter
    2, Pentecost predicted.

AMOS

Author
    The author was Amos.

Date
    Period covered and date written: about 760 BC. The length of the prophet's ministry is not known.

Theme
    Amos is the book of many judgments. A native of Judah, Amos was called to prophesy in Israel the coming judgment of God. His message was a call to repentance and a cry for justice.

Contents
    1—2, Prophecy of universal judgment; 3—6, Prophecy of Israel's judgment; 7—9, Symbols of Israel's condition.

Key Chapters
    5, A call for justice; 7, Amos defends his ministry.

OBADIAH

Author
    The author was Obadiah.

Date
   Period covered and date written: about 586 BC.

Theme
   Obadiah is the book of doom and deliverance. It pronounces doom on Edom for invading Judah while the Babylonians were destroying Jerusalem. In God's own time he will bring deliverance to Israel. Obadiah is the shortest book in the Old Testament.

Contents
   1:1-9, Doom on Edom; 1:10-14, Edom's sin against Jacob; 1:15-21, The day of the Lord.

Key Chapters
   Obadiah has only one chapter.

JONAH

Author
   The author appears to be Jonah.

Date
   Period covered and date written: Probably about 750 BC.

Theme
   Jonah is the book of God's mercy. The focus of His mercy is beyond Israel to the pagans of the world. The Ninevites' readiness to repent is seen as a contrast to Israel's resistance to God's call.

Contents
   1, Jonah's commission and flight; 2, Jonah's prayer; 3, Nineveh repents; 4, Jonah's hard lesson.

Key Chapters
   1, Jonah's flight and God's pursuit; 4, God's compassion toward all people.

MICAH

Author
   The author was Micah.

Date
   Period covered and date written: about 740 to 700 BC.

Theme
   Micah is the book of divine displeasure and delight. God is dis-

pleased with the false prophets, economic exploitation, and religious sham of both Israel and Judah. Therefore, judgment is coming. However, a deliverer will come from Bethlehem who will bring peace and blessing to the world.

Contents
1—3, The sins and sentence of Samaria and Judah; 4—5, Future hope for the remnant; 6—7, The divine lawsuit.

Key Chapters
4, Universal peace; 6, The Lord's requirements.

NAHUM

Author
The author was Nahum

Date
Period covered and date written: about 620 BC.

Theme
Nahum is the book of vengeance. Jonah reported the repentance of Nineveh, capital of Assyria. Nineveh then returned to its evil ways and threatened Judah. This raised the question, "Has God forgotten Judah?" The prophet Nahum provided the answer. "Nineveh will fall."

Contents
1, Judgment for God's enemies, comfort for God's people; 2 Nineveh attacked; 3, Nineveh destroyed.

Key Chapter
1, God's justice toward His people and His enemies.

HABAKKUK

Author
The author was Habakkuk.

Date
Period covered and date written: about 600 BC.

Theme
Habakkuk is the book of perplexity and vision. The prophet is perplexed by God's reluctance to judge Judah for its wickedness. God replies that Babylon will soon be the instrument of His wrath.

This raises a second problem. How can God allow pagan Babylon to punish Judah who is actually more righteous than Babylon? God answers that the just shall live by faith. The prophet then has a vision of the triumph of righteousness.

Contents
1, The prophet's problems; 2, God's solution; 3, The prophet's prayer.

Key Chapter
2, Living by faith when God seems unfaithful.

ZEPHANIAH

Author
The author was Zephaniah.

Date
Period covered and date written: about 625 BC.

Theme
Zephaniah is the book of the day of the Lord. Like the prophets before him, Zephaniah pictures the day of the Lord as a time of judgment and gloom. However, beyond judgment, he sees God's love and mercy resulting in universal salvation.

Contents
1, The coming day of the Lord; 2, Judgment against the nations; 3, Defeat and blessing for Jerusalem.

Key Chapter
3, All nations are blessed through the faithful remnant.

HAGGAI

Author
The author was Haggai.

Date
Period covered and date written: about 520 BC.

Theme
Haggai is the book of the second temple. The first exiles to return from captivity started rebuilding the temple but soon stopped the task. After sixteen years, Haggai calls them to complete the rebuilding. When they put God's work first, He will bless them materially and spiritually.

Contents
1:1-11, Israel's poverty explained; 1:12-15, The people respond; 2:1-19, Encouragement and promised blessing; 2:20-23, The promised ruler.

Key Chapter
2, God has unlimited blessings for the faithful.

ZECHARIAH

Author
The author was Zechariah. (Some assign 9—14 to a different author.)

Date
Period covered and date written: about 520 BC or later.

Theme
Zechariah is the book of visions of things present and final. The prophet links many earlier prophecies and future messianic events. Chapters 1 to 8 contain imagery from earlier writings. Chapters 9 to 14 find fulfillment in Christ.

Contents
1—6, Eight visions of future glory; 7—8, The prophet's message to Jerusalem; 9—14, The coming kingdom of God.

Key Chapters
4, The temple to be built by God's Spirit; 9, The Messiah arrives in Jerusalem; 14, God's universal kingdom.

MALACHI

Author
The author was Malachi.

Date
Period covered and date written: about 460 BC or later.

Theme
Malachi is the book of hope in the midst of darkness. About 80 years have passed since the temple was rebuilt and the promised blessings have not come. Both priests and people became discouraged and spiritually lax. The prophet again declares the coming Messiah. Prophecy now ceases until the coming of John the Baptist.

Contents
1:1-5, God's love for Israel; 1:6—2:16, Israel's disobedience to God; 2:17—3:6, The coming judgment; 3:7-12, Tithes and offerings; 3:13—4:3, A call for justice; 4:4-6, The Day of the Lord.

Key Chapters
2, Marriage and divorce; 3, Our giving and God's gifts.

MATTHEW

Author
The author was the Apostle Matthew.

Date
Period covered: about 4 BC to AD 30. Date written: between AD 65 and AD 90.

Theme
Matthew is the book of Jesus the King. This Gospel was written primarily for Jews and pictures Jesus as the Messiah prophesied in the Old Testament. Special emphasis is given to Jesus' teachings about the kingdom of heaven. The Gospel of Matthew is a fitting link between the Old and the New Testaments.

Contents
1—4, Birth and early ministry; 5—25, The teachings and ministry of Jesus (there are five alternating sections); 26—28, Death and resurrection.

Key Chapters
1—2, Jesus' birth and infancy; 5—7, The Sermon on the Mount; 25, Parables of judgment.

MARK

Author
The author was Mark (John Mark).

Date
Period covered: about AD 27 to 30. Date written: about AD 60 to 70 or earlier.

Theme
Mark is the book of Jesus the Servant of God. The focus of Mark, the shortest of the Gospels, is on the activity of Jesus. This Gospel was probably the first to be written.

Contents
1:1-13, Baptism and temptation; 1:14—9 Galilean ministry; 10, Perean ministry; 11—15, Passion week; 16, Resurrection.

Key Chapters
4, The parable of the sower; 6, Feeding the five thousand.

LUKE

Author
The author was Luke.

Date
Period covered: about 4 BC to AD 30. Date written: about AD 60 to 70.

Theme
Luke is the book of Jesus the Son of Man. Jesus is presented as the Savior of all men. He is pictured as having compassion for all people, especially the sick, the poor, and the social outcasts.

Contents
1—2, Birth and childhood; 3—4:13, John the Baptist and Jesus; 4:14—9:50, Galilean ministry; 9:51—19:44, Journey to Jerusalem; 19:45—21, Jerusalem ministry; 22—24, Passion and resurrection.

Key Chapters
2, Jesus' birth and childhood; 4, Jesus' ministry introduced; 10, The Good Samaritan; 15, The prodigal son.

JOHN

Author
The author was the Apostle John.

Date
Period covered: about AD 27 to 30. Date written: about AD 90.

Theme
John is the book of Jesus the Son of God. The stated purpose is to bring people to faith (20:30-31). Primary emphasis is placed on Jesus' sayings about Himself and the meaning of the events in His life. This Gospel is unique in its reporting of miracle "signs" and its reference to Jesus as the "I am."

Contents
1:1-18, Prologue; 1:19-51, Disciples called; 2—12, Public

ministry; 13—17, Private ministry with the disciples; 18—21, Passion and resurrection.

Key Chapters
3, The new birth; 6, The bread of life; 10, The good shepherd; 17, The High Priestly Prayer.

ACTS

Author
The author was Luke.

Date
Period covered: about AD 30 to 62. Date written: about AD 63.

Theme
Acts is the book of apostolic witnessing. The Gospel of Luke presents the witness of Jesus Christ. The story is continued in Acts which gives major attention to the witness of Peter and Paul. Through their ministry, the gospel moves from the center of Jewish life, Jerusalem, to the center of Roman life, Rome. This development was only possible through the power of the Holy Spirit.

Contents
1—7, The church begins at Jerusalem; 8—12, The spread from Jerusalem; 13—21:16, The missionary travels of Paul; 21:17—28, To Rome in chains.

Key Chapters
2, Pentecost; 7, The first martyr; 10, The gospel reaches Gentiles; 15, The Jerusalem Council; 28, Paul preaches at Rome.

ROMANS

Author
The author was Paul.

Date
Period covered and date written: about AD 57.

Theme
Romans is the book of justification by faith. The longest of Paul's Epistles, Romans has been called the most important book in the Bible. Paul wanted to visit Rome en route to Spain. He wrote this book to the church at Rome to report on his planned visit and explain the gospel he preached.

Contents
1—3, The gospel needed by everyone; 4—5, The gospel received by faith; 6—8, The gospel expressed in holy living; 9—11, The gospel and Israel; 12—16, The gospel shared with everyone.

Key Chapters
1, The gospel and man's need; 5, Christ offers forgiveness; 8, New life through the Holy Spirit; 12, Living the new life.

1 CORINTHIANS

Author
The author was Paul.

Date
Period covered and date written: about AD 54.

Theme
First Corinthians is the book of church order. The young church at Corinth faced many problems. Paul received reports that concerned him. Later the church asked Paul's advice on a number of issues. This Epistle is Paul's response. He introduces his discussion of their questions with the phrase, "Now concerning."

Contents
1—6, Errors of doctrine and practice; 7—14, Advice on current issues; 15, The resurrection; 16, Concluding concerns.

Key Chapters
2, Spiritual wisdom; 12, Spiritual gifts; 13, The love chapter; 15, The resurrection of the body.

2 CORINTHIANS

Author
The author was Paul.

Date
Period covered and date written: about AD 56.

Theme
Second Corinthians is the book regarding the ministry. False teachers attempted to undermine Paul's apostolic authority. This Epistle defends his authority and his ministry. It also commends

the church at Corinth for their response to his warnings and teachings. Second Corinthians is Paul's most personal letter.

Contents
1—2, Paul's recent activities; 3—7, Paul answers his critics; 8—9, The offering for the Jerusalem Christians; 10—13, Paul's apostolic authority.

Key Chapters
5, The ministry of reconciliation; 9, Motivation for Christian giving; 11, Paul's personal sacrifice for the gospel.

GALATIANS

Author
The author was Paul.

Date
Period covered: about AD 33 to 48. Date written: about AD 48.

Theme
Galatians is the book of law and grace. After Paul founded churches in the province of Galatia, certain Jewish teachers taught that faith was not enough for salvation. They insisted that Gentiles needed to observe Jewish laws to be Christians. Paul wrote to defend his message of salvation by grace.

Contents
1—2, The authority of Paul's gospel; 3—4, Paul's gospel defended; 5—6, True freedom.

Key Chapters
3, Righteousness through faith; 5, The nature and limits of freedom.

EPHESIANS

Author
The author was Paul.

Date
Period covered and date written: about AD 61 while a prisoner in Rome.

Theme
Ephesians is the book of the heavenlies. Paul was called to evan-

gelize the Gentiles but he could never accept a divided church. Ephesians shows God's plan to unite people of all nations in Christ. In Christ we now sit in heavenly places. All believers are therefore one in Christ's body.

Contents
1—3, The church as envisioned by Christ; 4—5, The church in society; 6, The Christian's warfare.

Key Chapters
2, New life in Christ; 5, Mutual subjection of husband and wife; 6, The Christian's enemy and armor.

PHILIPPIANS

Author
The author was Paul.

Date
Period covered and date written: about AD 62 while a prisoner in Rome.

Theme
Philippians is the book of joy and rejoicing. This very personal letter was written to believers he knew intimately and loved deeply. His fatherly concern is quite evident. Most striking is the note of joy in spite of harsh circumstances.

Contents
1, Paul's circumstances; 2, The example of Christ; 3—4, Warnings and exhortations.

Key Chapters
2, Christ's example of humility; 4, Rejoice in the Lord.

COLOSSIANS

Author
The author was Paul.

Date
Period covered and date written: about AD 61 while a prisoner in Rome.

Theme
Colossians is the book of the preeminence of Christ. The Chris-

tians at Colossae added to Christianity, pagan philosophy, and the worship of angels. Paul points out that Christ is above everything in the universe. They cannot add to Christ but they can take away from His supreme position.

Contents
1, The excellence of Christ; 2, The failure of false teachings; 3—4, Advice on Christian living.

Key Chapters
1, The preeminence of Christ; 3, The new life in Christ.

1 THESSALONIANS

Author
The author was Paul.

Date
Period covered and date written: about AD 50.

Theme
First Thessalonians is the book of the second coming of Christ. This letter was written in response to a report Paul received regarding the church at Thessalonica. In the letter, Paul expressed his joy concerning the good news. He also provided teaching to meet some of their needs, especially misunderstandings about the second coming of Christ.

Contents
1—3, Paul's relationship to the church; 4—5, Paul's exhortations to the church.

Key Chapters
1, Vital Christianity; 4, The coming of the Lord.

2 THESSALONIANS

Author
The author was Paul.

Date
Period covered and date written: about AD 50.

Theme
Second Thessalonians is the book of the day of the Lord. This letter was written a short time after 1 Thessalonians. Paul again

commended them for their spiritual growth and corrected certain false ideas about the day of the Lord.

Contents
1, Thanksgiving and encouragement; 2, The day of the Lord; 3, Church discipline.

Key Chapter
2, Events preceding the return of Christ.

1 TIMOTHY

Author
The author was Paul.

Date
Period covered and date written: about AD 63.

Theme
First Timothy is the book of pastoral work. Paul seemed to know that his ministry would soon end and that Timothy would carry more responsibility for the churches. This Epistle contains instructions about church organization and a warning to avoid false teachers.

Contents
1, The charge to Timothy; 2, Public worship; 3, Qualifications for the ministry; 4, Dealing with apostasy; 5—6, Instructions to church groups.

Key Chapters
4, Encouragement to a young minister; 6, Instructions to a young minister.

2 TIMOTHY

Author
The author was Paul.

Date
Period covered and date written: about AD 64.

Theme
Second Timothy is the book of loyalty to God and truth. The end had come. Paul was again in prison facing imminent death. In

his last Epistle, he stated his readiness to die for Christ and his encouragement to those who continue to carry the torch of truth.

Contents
   1, A call for courage; 2, A call for steadfastness; 3—4:5, A call to preach the Word; 4:6-22, Paul's last words.

Key Chapters
   3, Life in the last days; 4, Waiting for the crown.

TITUS

Author
   The author was Paul.

Date
   Period covered and date written: about AD 63.

Theme
   Titus is the book of sound doctrine. Paul wrote to Titus giving him final instruction on dealing with the church in Crete. The two areas of concern were leadership and divine truth.

Contents
   1, The qualifications of leaders; 2, The message for ministers; 3, A call to Christian living.

Key Chapter
   2, Christians living in a pagan society.

PHILEMON

Author
   The author was Paul.

Date
   Period covered and date written: about AD 61 while a prisoner in Rome.

Theme
   Philemon is the book of Christian forgiveness. Through the ministry of Paul, Onesimus, a runaway slave, was converted. Paul sent him back to his owner with this letter urging that he be accepted back as a brother in Christ.

Contents
1-7 Greetings and thanksgiving; 8-20, Paul pleads for Onesimus; 21-25, Personal matters.

Key Chapter
Philemon has only one chapter.

HEBREWS

Author
The author is not named.

Date
Period covered and date written: about AD 67.

Theme
Hebrews is the book of better things. The book was written to Jewish Christians who were turning back to Judaism. Jesus Christ was shown to be far better than the Old Testament priesthood and sacrificial system.

Contents
1—4:13, The superiority of Christ; 4:14—10:18, Christ, the eternal High Priest; 10:19—12, A call to a life of faith; 13, Personal messages.

Key Chapters
1, Christ brings God's final word; 5, Christ our High Priest; 9, The new covenant; 10, The new privileges; 11, The achievements of faith.

JAMES

Author
The author was James, the brother of Jesus.

Date
Period covered and date written: about AD 60 or earlier.

Theme
James is the book of practical Christian living. The emphasis is not evangelism but rather discipleship. James shows that Christianity has both blessings and duties. Genuine faith will always effect life.

Contents
1, God's call to pure religion; 2—5, Nine tests of pure religion.

Key Chapters
1, Be doers of the Word; 3, The untamable tongue; 5, Patience and prayer.

1 PETER

Author
The author was Peter.

Date
Period covered and date written: about AD 63.

Theme
First Peter is the book of precious things. Peter wrote to Christians who were young in their faith and who were facing persecution for that faith. His message focused on their rich blessings in Christ and encouragement to faithful living.

Contents
1—2:10, A call to Holy living; 2:11—3:12, A call to submissive living; 3:13—5:14, A call to follow the examples of Christ.

Key Chapters
2, God's new people; 4, Living faithfully under difficult circumstances.

2 PETER

Author
The author was Peter.

Date
Period covered and date written: about AD 65.

Theme
Second Peter is the book of the last things. This Epistle was written near the end of Peter's life. The two primary concerns are righteous living and the certainty of Christ's return.

Contents
1, The word of truth; 2, False teachers; 3, The coming of the Lord.

Key Chapters
    1, The sure word of Scripture; 3, The sure return of Christ.

1 JOHN

Author
    The author was the Apostle John.

Date
    Period covered and date written: about AD 90 to 95.

Theme
    First John is the book of assurance or of reassurance. The letter is written to reassure believers about their faith in Christ. False teachers had urged Christians to add pagan philosophy (Gnosticism) to Christianity. The result of this addition was tragic. It led to loose living and immorality. It also led to a rejection of the humanity of Christ. The heart of Christianity was thus removed and those who had faith believed in vain.

Contents
    1—2, God is light; 3—4, God is love; 5, The Christian's assurance.

Key Chapters
    1, Walking in the light; 3, Walking in love; 5, Assurance of salvation.

2 JOHN

Author
    The author was the Apostle John.

Date
    Period covered and date written: about AD 90 to 95.

Theme
    Second John is the book of truth. This epistle warns against fellowshiping with false teachers. Christians are called to love, truth, and obedience. False teachings undermine these virtues.

Contents
    1-6, Walk in love and truth; 7-13, Follow sound doctrine.

Key Chapter
    Second John has only one chapter.

3 JOHN

Author
The author was the Apostle John.

Date
Period covered and date written: about AD 90 to 95.

Theme
Third John is the book of fellow-helpers. John wrote to his friend Gaius to commend him for entertaining traveling preachers. Christian hospitality was very necessary in the life of the apostolic church.

Contents
1-4, Follow the truth; 5-8, Practice hospitality; 9-14, Leaders contrasted.

Key Chapter
Third John has only one chapter.

JUDE

Author
The author was Jude, a brother of Jesus.

Date
Period covered and date written: about AD 80.

Theme
Jude is the book of contending for the faith. False teachers were undermining the believers by their immoral character and conduct. Jude warns of certain judgment for the immoral. God alone can keep them from falling into such sins.

Contents
1-4, Hold fast to the faith; 5-11, Examples of God's judgment; 12-16, The emptiness of false Christians; 17-23, False and genuine Christians; 24-25, A doxology of praise.

Key Chapter
Jude has only one chapter.

REVELATION

Author
The author was the Apostle John.

Date

Period covered and date written: about AD 95.

Theme

Revelation is the book of last things. While it reveals final world events it also reveals the One who controls those events. The book is the revelation of Jesus Christ. It is a revelation of Christ Himself and a revelation from Christ of events yet to take place.

Contents

1, The Christ of Revelation; 2—3, Christ's lordship over the church; 4—5, Christ's lordship over history; 6—11, Christ's body and Satan in conflict; 12—14, Christ and Satan in conflict; 15—20, Christ's victory over His enemies; 21—22, Christ in eternity.

Key Chapters

2—3, Letters to the seven churches; 4—5, The throne and the Lamb; 20, Satan's doom; 21, The new heaven and the new earth.

QUESTIONS FOR REFLECTION OR DISCUSSION

1. In the introduction to this chapter, three ways are suggested for using the capsules of information. Which approach do you plan to follow?

2. What new insights did you gain about the groupings of the books of the Bible?

3. Have you memorized the books of the Bible? If not, I recommend that you do.

12

Resources for Further Study

Throughout this book, I have been emphasizing the study of the Bible itself rather than books about the Bible. Therefore, it may be surprising to find a final chapter on resources to be used in your continued Bible study. Do not forget that this book is intended to help you study the Bible for yourself and that there are many other books that have the same purpose. If this book has been helpful, some of them will be helpful too.

Books of this type can be considered tools for Bible study. Every carpenter has at least the basic tools such as a hammer, saw, square, level, and pencil. These are necessary for building. Likewise, the Bible student needs basic Bible study tools. Without them, the scope of study will be limited.

The following books are suggested as study aids. The listing is not comprehensive. There are many other excellent books, too many to be included in this brief chapter. These listed are some that I have found helpful. I recommend them to you. Most of them are available at a religious bookstore.

A Suitable Bible

Since the primary tool for Bible study is the Bible, it is important that yours be easy to read and to understand. Among the many translations available, here are a few to be considered. Then pick the one most suitable for you.

> *Good News Bible* (GNB, 1976, American Bible Society, Collins, Nelson). People who find most translations difficult to understand will have a pleasant surprise when they start reading the Good News Bible. It is both very readable and very close to the original languages of Hebrew and Greek. International persons who have studied English should be able to understand this translation. Paperback editions are quite inexpensive.
>
> *New International Version* (NIV, 1978, Zondervan). For over ten years, an international team of evangelical scholars worked on this translation. They emphasized stating in clear English the original Scriptures without losing literary quality. They attempted to prepare a totally new translation, not a revision of the King James Version.
>
> *Revised Standard Version* (RSV, 1952, several publishers). This version is a revision of the 1901 American Standard Version. The translators attempted to preserve the qualities of the King James Version which are so desirable for public and private worship. The RSV has found wide acceptance by both Protestants and Catholics. It is the text for many Bible commentaries.
>
> *King James Version* (KJV, 1611, many publishers). The English language made major changes since the seventeenth century and the KJV received periodic updatings into the 1800s. In spite of its age, sales remain the highest of any single translation.

A Bible Atlas

Christianity is a historic faith. It is based on the activity of God for man's salvation. The Bible is a historic book. It reports the actions and messages of God to His people in Palestine. Good maps are essential for understanding the Bible's message. Such maps are found in a Bible atlas.

> *Atlas of the Bible Lands* edited by Harry Thomas Frank
> (1977, Hammond Incorporated). This booklet contains
> excellent maps and pictures of the Bible lands. They cover
> the entire period of biblical history from the time of the
> Patriarchs to the New Testament era. There are maps of
> the Middle East, of Palestine, and the city of Jerusalem.

A *Bible Handbook*

A Bible handbook brings together a wealth of material
about the Bible, about life in Bible times, and summary information about the books of the Bible. A number of good
handbooks are available. Among these are the following:

> *Halley's Bible Handbook* by Henry H. Halley (1965, Zon-
> dervan). Beginning as a 16-page leaflet in 1924, this hand-
> book has grown to 864 pages. It is designed for the
> average Bible reader who has few study resources. With
> over three million copies in print, it is considered the most
> used guidebook to the Bible in the world today.

> *Eerdman's Handbook to the Bible* edited by David
> Alexander and Pat Alexander (1973 Wm. B. Eerdmans
> Publishing Company). This handbook presents the latest
> insights of biblical scholarship and archaeology in a style
> that is very readable. Its four main sections cover general
> information about the Bible, the Old and New Testa-
> ments, and key themes and doctrines of the Scriptures.
> Colored pictures and maps add to the attractiveness of the
> book. This book was a primary resource for me in writing
> chapters 10 and 11.

A *One-Volume Commentary*

The purpose of a Bible commentary is to explain the
meaning of the Scriptures. A one-volume commentary is
adequate for general Bible study. Large sets of commentaries are available for detailed study.

> *The New Bible Commentary: Revised* edited by D. Guthrie
> and J. A. Motyer (1970, Wm. B. Eerdmans Publishing

Company). This commentary was first published in 1953 as a distinctively evangelical work. It was widely used by lay students and pastors. The revised edition contains many new articles and much additional material. It represents the combined work of 51 scholars making it one of the best one-volume commentaries available.

Matthew Henry's Commentary by Matthew Henry (1961, Zondervan Publishing House). Written over 250 years ago, it has been the most widely used of all commentaries. Originally published in five volumes, the one-volume edition retains its helpful insights in condensed form. According to Dr. Wilbur M. Smith, it is "the greatest devotional commentary ever written."

A Bible Dictionary

The Bible contains many unfamiliar terms with significant meaning and many familiar terms whose full meanings we may not know. A Bible dictionary can unlock hidden treasures in most biblical words.

The New Bible Dictionary edited by J. D. Douglas (1962, Wm. B. Eerdmans Publishing Company). The areas covered, in addition to biblical terms, include the geography, history, and customs of Bible lands. Articles discuss major doctrines such as justification, salvation, revelation, inspiration, and holiness.

Pictorial Bible Dictionary by Merrill C. Tenney (1967, Zondervan Publishing House). Like other similar dictionaries, this volume focuses on Bible history, geography, chronology, and biographies. The distinctive feature is over 700 carefully selected pictures.

The International Standard Bible Encyclopedia, General editor, James Orr (1952, Wm. B. Eerdmans Publishing Company). This five-volume encyclopedia has been a standard resource for Bible students and pastors for many years. The set is presently being revised.

A Bible Concordance

When you wish to locate a particular Bible verse, all you need is to know a key word in the verse and to have a concordance. The basic feature of a concordance is a listing of the various verses containing key Bible terms. Many Bibles have a brief concordance at the back of the book. There are three familiar Bible concordances available based on the King James Version of the Bible. All are available in either a hard-cover or a paperback edition.

> *The Exhaustive Concordance of the Bible* by James Strong (1947, Abingdon Press). This concordance is truly exhaustive in that it lists every word in the Bible and every passage where that word occurs. It also indicates the Hebrew or Greek term behind the English word and contains a comparative concordance.

> *Analytical Concordance to the Bible* by Robert Young (1964, Wm. B. Eerdmans Publishing Company). In addition to listing the references containing key words, this concordance is analytical in that it identifies the various meanings of key words and their theological implications.

> *Crudens Complete Concordance* by Alexander Cruden (1949, Zondervan Publishing House). Even though this concordance is the smallest of the three, it is adequate for most needs. It provides an alphabetical index to all of the key words in the Bible and an index to the proper names and their meanings.

A Bible Background Book

Since the Bible was written in the Middle East and in a particular historical setting, books dealing with the general background are valuable aids to understanding. Many such books are available. Here are several that I have found helpful.

> *Understanding the Bible* by John R. W. Stott (1972, Regal Books Division, Gospel Light Publications). Stott's writ-

ings abound in fresh insights and practical applications. This paperback book deals with areas such as the purpose, land, story, and authority of the Bible.

The New Testament: An Historical and Analytic Survey by Merrill C. Tenney (1953, Wm. B. Eerdmans Publishing Company). In addition to a survey of the New Testament books, Tenney discusses the political, social, economic, and religious worlds of the New Testament era. He also discusses the origin of Judaism and Jewish religious life.

Old Testament Times by R. K. Harrison (1970, Wm. B. Eerdmans Publishing Company). Like most books dealing with the Old Testament, this book takes the reader into the unfamiliar world of the past. The people and places sound strange to our ears but they were familiar to God's people in the Old Testament. As the title suggests, this book covers the general Old Testament story in its setting rather than a discussion of the individual books.

A Guide to Systematic Bible Study

In chapter 8 you were introduced to systematic Bible study, sometimes called inductive Bible study. This introduction may have seemed very detailed. Actually, it was a simplified form. If the approach had value for you, I would recommend your continued study of the method.

The Joy of Discovery in Bible Study by Oletta Wald (1975, Augsburg Publishing House). In two main sections, the author first explains the principles of inductive study and then illustrates the various steps used by this method. Many study illustrations are based on the Book of James.

Personal Bible Study by William C. Lincoln (1975, Bethany Fellowship). This book presents an excellent discussion of inductive study but it has fewer illustrations of the method than *The Joy of Discovery*. Both authors were introduced to inductive study by Dr. Robert A. Traina at Biblical Seminary in New York. Both have written a book to introduce the method to lay students.

QUESTIONS FOR REFLECTION AND DISCUSSION

1. What Bible study aids have been most valuable to you in your study of the Bible? What recent insights have you discovered?

2. Which book or books identified in this chapter would be most helpful to your present Bible study? Make a priority list for yourself. It will be a good guide for the books you buy.

John R. Martin is registrar and associate professor of church ministry at Eastern Mennonite Seminary, Harrisonburg, Virginia.

He received the BA degree from Eastern Mennonite College (1954) and the ThB (1955) and BD (1960) degrees from Goshen Biblical Seminary. He completed the first unit of Clinical Pastoral Education at Lancaster General Hospital, Lancaster, Pennsylvania (1971) and earned the ThM degree from Eastern Baptist Theological Seminary (1972).

During early seminary studies, Martin served as a mission pastor at Walkerton, Indiana. This was followed by a three-year part-time pastorate in a mission congregation in Washington, D.C. From 1961 to 1971, he pastored the Neffsville Mennonite Church, Neffsville, Pennsylvania. He also served as an area overseer in his conference district. In 1971, he joined the Bible faculty at Eastern Mennonite College and taught there until 1978.

Martin has served as executive secretary of National Service Board for Religious Objectors, Washington, D.C.; director of I-W Services for Mennonite Board of Missions, Elkhart, Indiana; a member of the board of trustees of Eastern Mennonite College; and president of Mennonite Broadcasts, Inc. (now Media Ministries), Harrisonburg, Virginia. He is presetnly a member of the Mennonite Board of Congregational Ministries.

He is the author of *Divorce and Remarriage: A Perspective for Counseling* (Herald Press) and of numerous articles.

A native of Harrisonburg, John was sixth in a closely knit family of nine children. He married Marian Landis of Blooming Glen, Pennsylvania, in 1956. They are members of the Park View Mennonite Church, where John is an elder.